AUBREY BEARDSLEY

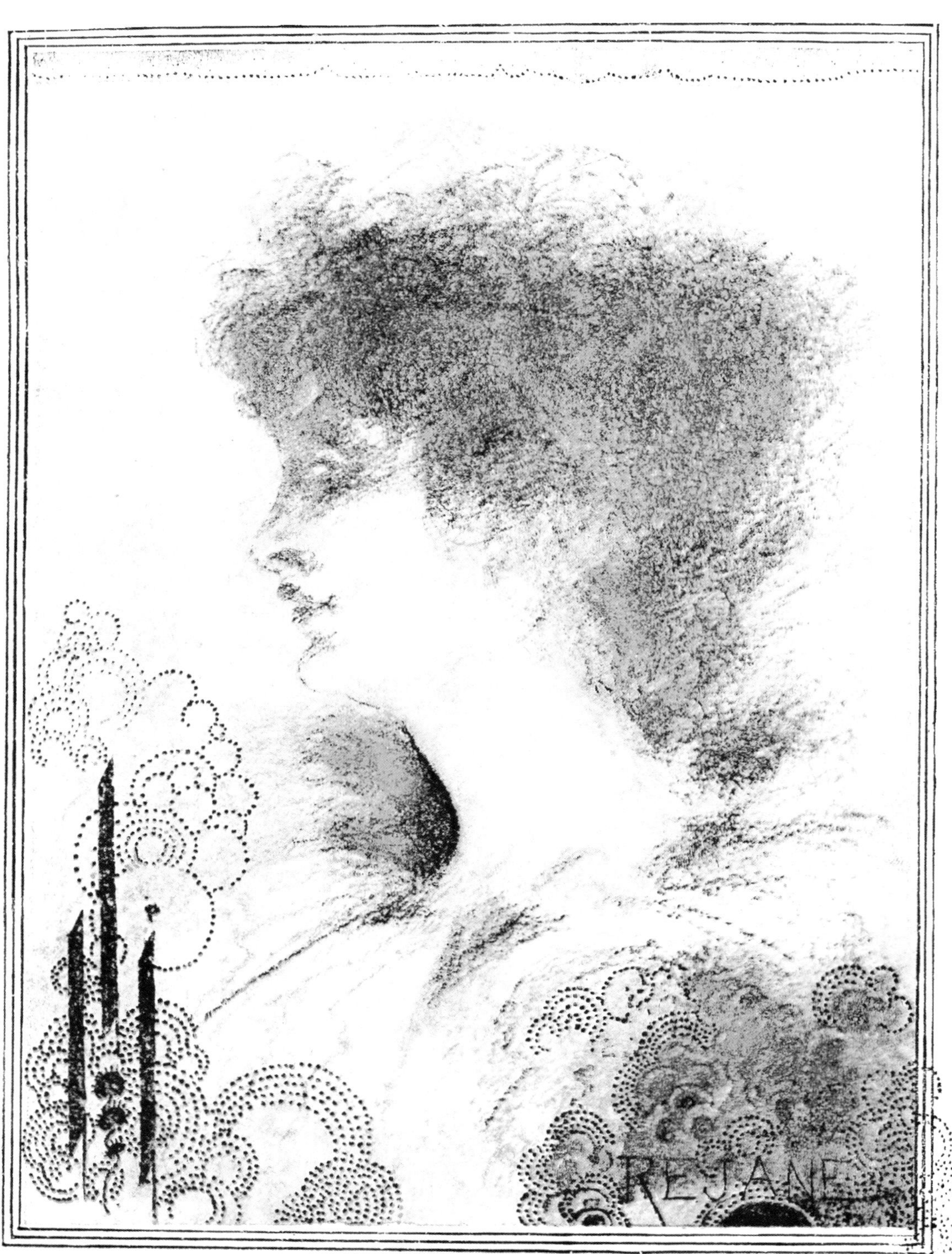
REJANE

AUBREY BEARDSLEY

Sixty Selected Drawings

WITH AN ESSAY BY BRIDGET ELLIOTT

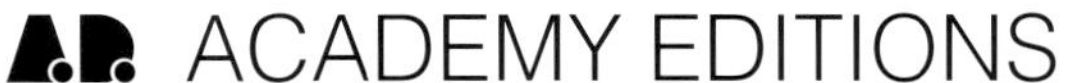

ACADEMY EDITIONS

Front cover: The Peacock Skirt, *Salomé*; Title page:
Venus, *Venus and Tannhäusser*; Back cover: Merlin,

First published in Great Britain in 1995 by
ACADEMY EDITIONS
an imprint of

ACADEMY GROUP LTD
42 Leinster Gardens, London W2 3AN
Member of the VCH Publishing Group

ISBN: 1 85490 429 9

Distributed to the trade in the United States of America by
NATIONAL BOOK NETWORK INC
4720 Boston Way, Lanham, Maryland 20706

Printed and bound in Singapore

98-0177

CONTENTS

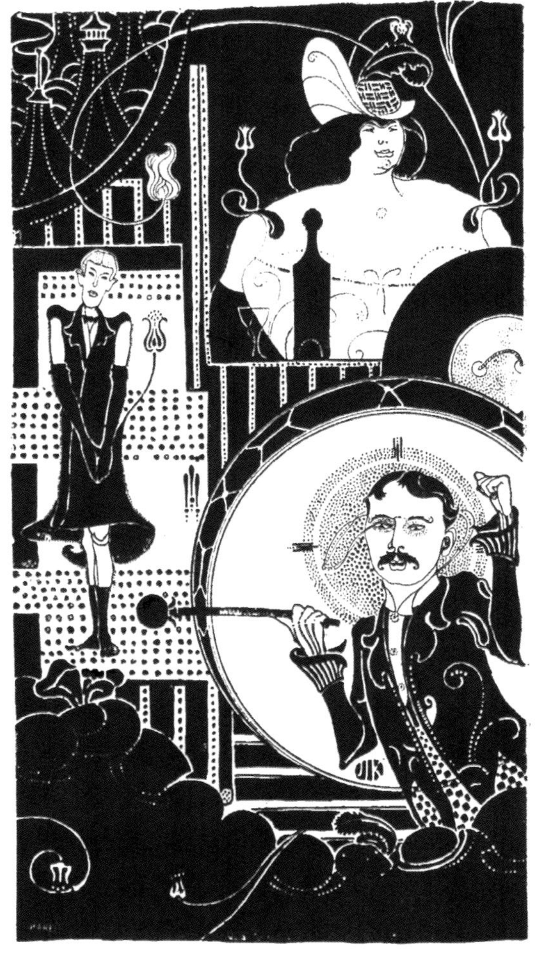
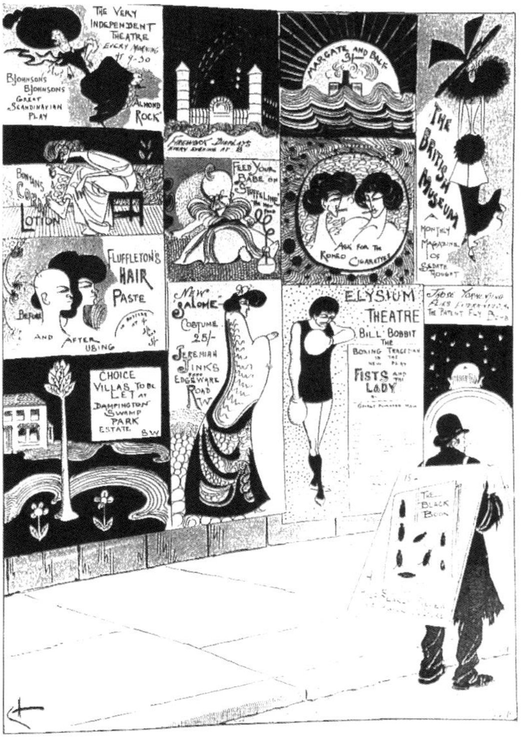

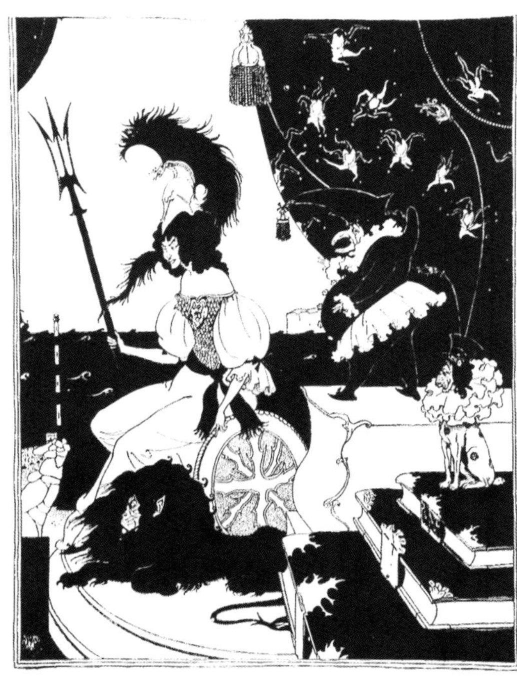
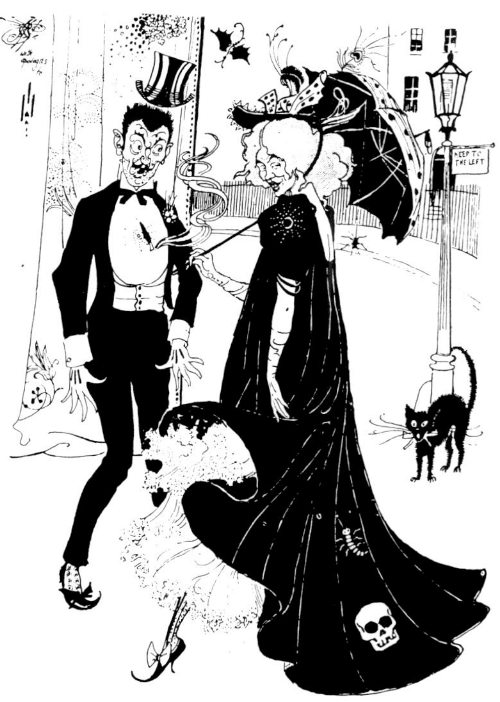

FROM ABOVE, LEFT TO RIGHT: Fig 1, An Illustration to the Gospel of *To-Day* by Baudrey Weirdsley, To-Day, *Sept 22, 1894*; *Fig 2*, The New School of Poster, What it May Come to *by CH [Charles Harrison]*, Pall Mall Budget, *May 10, 1894*; *Fig 3*, Britannia à la Beardsley *by ETR [Edward Reed]*, Punch Almanac, *1895*; *Fig 4*, How It Is Done (An Art Recipe), Punch, *July 28, 1894*

AUBREY BEARDSLEY AS PERFORMER
FIN-DE-SIÈCLE OR *ENTR'ACTE?*

Whether or not they liked his work, many cultural critics of the 1890s felt Aubrey Beardsley's distinctive black-and-white style symbolised the controversial new forms of literature, drama, music and art which were being produced by a *fin-de-siècle* generation just reaching maturity.

In 1896, the writer Max Beerbohm summed things up by claiming that he belonged to 'the Beardsley period.'[1] The fact that the twenty-six year old Beardsley had recently been fired from his position as the art editor of the infamous *Yellow Book* made him an irresistible target for satirists and gossips. Avidly following such cultural developments was the weekly periodical, *To-Day*, which had already kept its readers amused for several years with a steady stream of cartoons depicting the artist. Two years earlier, one of *To-Day's* cartoons, *An Illustration of the Gospel of To-Day by Baudry Weirdsley* (fig 1), had portrayed the artist in the left middle-ground, cross-dressed as the famous French café-singer, Yvette Guilbert. Like so many others, Beardsley greatly admired Guilbert and asked his publisher to send her a copy of his *Rape of the Lock* (plates 14-19) when she performed at London's famous Empire music-hall in May of 1896. Both Guilbert's typical pose and characteristic long black gloves would have been recognised readily by *To-Day's* readers, who had probably seen numerous publicity pictures of the singer.[2] Equally unmistakeable was the superimposed figure of Beardsley with his gaunt physique, large protruding ears and straight, bluntly-cut fringe of hair. Readers would also have identified Beardsley's picture, *The Fat Woman*, in the upper right since it had been reproduced in an earlier article from a May issue entitled 'The New Master of Art: Mr Aubrey Beardsley.'[3] The bold juxtaposition of black and white spaces, the profusion of checked patterning and decorative dotting, as well as the long curving tendrils of flowery foliage were all borrowed from Beardsley, as was his famous 'trademark' (consisting of three vertical lines and three dots) which appears near the lower edge of his skirt.[4] Significantly, for our purposes, the cartoon placed Beardsley and his illustrations in the realm of popular entertainment, forming part of some bizarre music-hall or cabaret act introduced by a chairman or band-leader whose delicate features and curling moustache, eyebrows and hair physically resembled Beardsley's friend, Arthur Symons. The image of Symons as the showman who introduces Beardsley was particularly apt since it was generally held that Symons's celebrated article, 'The Decadent Movement in Literature', published in *Harper's New Monthly Magazine* in November of 1893, had brought the work of the French decadent writers, Mallarmé, Huysmans, and Verlaine to the attention of the English general public.[5]

A few years later, Symons himself had much to say about the theatrical qualities of Beardsley who, he felt, closely resembled Paul Verlaine's character, Pierrot gamin:

> Pierrot is passionate; but he does not believe in great passions . . . He knows that his face is powdered, and if he sobs, it is without tears; and it is hard to distinguish, under the chalk, if the grimace which twists his mouth awry is more laughter or mockery. He knows that he is condemned to be always in public, that emotion would be supremely out of keeping with his costume, that he must remember to be fantastic if he would not be merely ridiculous. So he becomes exquisitely false . . . [6]

According to Symons, this image of the artist as a somewhat jaded and ultimately tragic performer embodied the aesthetic disposition of a new *fin-de-siècle* art which owed its origins to the revival of Watteau and the artistic experiments of Manet, Degas and Whistler, as well as to the popular illustrated comic newspapers and posters of Cheret, Willette and Lautrec. Above all, this new hybrid art needed dramatic effects because it was, as Symons pointed out:

> meant for the street, for people who are walking fast. It comes into competition with the newspapers, with the music-halls; half contemptuously it popularizes itself; and, with real qualities and a real measure of good intention, finds itself forced to seek for sharp, sudden, arresting means of expression . . . And this art, this art of the day and hour competes not merely with the appeal and the popularity of the theatrical spectacle, but directly with theatrical methods, the methods of stage illusion.[7]

In this passage Symons draws attention to the commercial context of Beardsley's art which fully exploited the new mechanical photographic engraving process (developed in the 1880s and in widespread use in the 1890s) that enabled drawings to be quickly mass-produced for book publishers and periodical editors. This new form of 'process' illustration eliminated the need for time-consuming engravings, since artists' designs were photographed directly onto metal plates by a rising number of speciality firms such as the Swan Electric Engraving Company and Carl Hentchel. What had previously taken weeks and months for an engraver could now be done within hours.[8] The new ease of photographic reproduction increased the demand for high-quality pen-and-ink illustrators who now negotiated directly with publishers. In this sense, as Rodney Shewan has observed, Beardsley's career was 'well-timed' since it was 'doubtful that any preceding decade . . . could have accommodated so readily an artist of such limited technique and startling originality.'[9] In effect, Beardsley deliberately developed an elegant yet simple black-and-white style which was both cost-effective and eye-catching. It was precisely these qualities which were satirised in Charles Harrison's cartoon of the new commercial art entitled *The New School of Poster: What It May Come To* (fig 2) which was published in the *Pall Mall Budget* in May of 1894. In this instance, Harrison targets the work of both Dudley Hardy and Aubrey Beardsley as two of the best known graphic artists of that decade. At the upper right and left, Dudley Hardy's fashionable 'girls of the period' are parodied, while across the bottom register Beardsley's designs are mockingly recycled. In the poster at the lower left, Harrison reworked the stylised streams of water, trees and flowers from Beardsley's design for the third chapter of Book III of *Le Mort Darthur* (plate 25) into a poster advertising suburban villas of the cheap and nasty variety, at least judging from their insalubrious location. Next to the poster for the villas is an advertisement for costumes drawn from Beardsley's The Peacock Skirt (plate 1), one of his better known illustrations for Oscar Wilde's controversial play, *Salomé*, which was published by John Lane in 1893. Further visual jokes are made about the *Yellow Book*, which turns into a bug-infested *Black Book*, and George Bernard Shaw's play, *Arms and the Man*, which becomes a boxing match entitled *Fists and the Lady*, illustrated à la Beardsley.[10] Here, the most advanced avant-garde art and drama of the period are associated with the shoddy products and amusements of industrial mass culture.

Such comparisons, which were typically drawn in the nineties, warrant further consideration. Like so many others during this decade, Harrison embraces a rhetoric of the new, a term that was frequently applied to drama, literature, art, criticism, journalism, hedonism, paganism, socialism, imperialism and women. As the critic HD Traill noted in his study, *The New Fiction and Other Essays* (1897), 'Not to be 'new' is, in these days, to be nothing . . .'[11] However, if the new was all important, it was not always clear what it meant. In many instances it referred to products, trends, and fashions that were sold to consumers as the 'latest' or 'newest' by a rapidly expanding advertising industry. A steadily growing per capita income throughout the last half of the nineteenth century was generating an increasingly consumer-oriented economy. The term also applied to cultural goods (eg books, magazines, posters) produced with new technologies such as 'process' illustration and industrial pulp paper and disseminated quickly to unprecedented numbers of readers and viewers via modern communication networks and franchises such as the railway bookstalls of WH Smith.

When it came to the avant-garde, the new often signified a style and content that criticised the predominance of mainstream bourgeois values. For example, 'philistine' critics perceived such criticisms in the plays of Ibsen and Shaw, the music of Wagner, the writings of Wilde and Symons and the illustrations of Beardsley, to cite only a few names. Such forms of avant-garde 'newness' were often seen as unnecessarily sensational and shocking because they usually violated the accepted moral and social codes of the middle-classes. From this perspective, the new was the *cause célèbre* of various deviant subcultures whose political perspectives could range from a reactionary decadence to a visionary socialism, although any one individual or group probably embodied a number of curiously contradictory positions. It should be stressed that there were constant slippages between these different sorts of 'newness'. In the case of 'New Women' writers for instance, the new referred not only to their feminist promotion of such issues as a woman's right to work, hold property, receive equal pay and gain access to safe and reliable birth control, but also to their sensational themes, such as adultery and illegitimacy, as well as to the fact that their books were being published in cheap editions and read by a new constituency of 'half-educated' lower-middle-class women working as clerks and shop-assistants.[12] One of the things that makes the 1890s so fascinating (and relevant for the 1990s) was the widespread perception that the period was one of cultural crisis, occasioned, at least in part, by the advent of new technologies, the rise of a new type of public and the resulting erosion of traditional cultural forms and values. As increased leisure time and cultural literacy were extended to members of the lower-middle and working classes (after the Education Act of

1870), these groups became increasingly involved in the consumption of appealing and affordable mass-produced cultural commodities. Typical examples of the new cultural fare included the lavish entertainment of the syndicated music-hall chains and the light, amusing and gossipy chatter of penny journals such as *Tit-Bits,* which was soon selling hundreds of thousands of copies after its launch in 1881. By the middle of the nineties, a dramatic lowering of periodical and book prices meant that reading material could be purchased directly by members of the middle and lower-middle classes instead of being borrowed from circulating libraries such as Mudie's, which generally boycotted anything racy or controversial. Many conservative cultural critics feared the undermining of middle-class cultural standards would lead to political confrontation and social decay as ever-increasing numbers of outsiders (women, homosexuals, racial and social minorities, and members of the working-classes) began to assert their rights. Determined to repel such threats and jubilant after the sentencing of Oscar Wilde in 1895, the conservative critic, Harry Quilter, prophesied a brighter cultural future and a return to traditional values:

> I believe that the day will come, and that very shortly, when the present revolt against belief and modesty will cease to be a distinguishing mark of our art, our literature, and our journalism. I believe that we shall cease to imitate the worst vices of our French neighbours . . . I believe that sensational journalism has had its day, and that the level of the servants' hall is that to which it is doomed quickly to descend. I believe that novelists will soon not dare to publish, what they certainly would not dare to speak. I believe that critics will be afraid to praise such production. I believe that editors will be ashamed to employ the critics who do. I believe that poets will recur to the old beauties of the world, which are *not* identified with what we used to call vice and blasphemy. I believe that painters will find better subjects than are now furnished them in East-End public-houses, and West-End music-halls. And I believe that . . . our girls will no longer imitate our manners and our costume, but be content with their own, which are, after all, infinitely better; and that our men will no longer struggle after a pretence of effeminacy which sits upon them extremely ill. And lastly, I believe that . . . there will come back into the world some substitute for the old faith in God . . . [13]

Such widely articulated conservative points of view were reinforced in 1895 by the English translation of Max Nordau's *Degeneration* (originally published in German in 1892) which argued that nearly all of the new artistic tendencies (including William Morris, the Pre-Raphaelites, Oscar Wilde and the Symbolists in England, as well as Wagner, Ibsen, Huysmans, Manet and the Impressionists on the Continent) were the product of a diseased genius which stemmed from racial degeneration.

Critics like Quilter were quick to point out that Beardsley's illustrations were by far the most evil and pernicious examples of the new 'Anglo-Gallic school' of art. Condemning the modern journalism of the illustrated press which was 'daily vulgarising England,' Quilter urged other critics to denounce Beardsley's work and stem the decadent tide before it was too late. Warning of what was at stake, he could not resist speculating:

X

Just fancy a nation of Beardsleys! Conceive of politics, commerce, law, and religion approached from this standpoint, applied in this manner. And yet, why not? Art is, we are told with a sickening reiteration, but a reflection of life; why should we not have a Beardsley bishop addressing a Beardsley congregation, or say, a Mr Gully à la Beardsley, reproving an emasculated House of Commons?[14]

Edward Reed, one of *Punch's* leading cartoonists, developed this theme in his *Britannia à la Beardsley*, published in the *Punch Almanac* for 1895 (fig 3). Here, Britannia is shown in the guise of a Beardsley woman with dark curling hair, sensual lips, heavy thighs and hips as well as half-closed eyes (note her resemblance to the French actress Réjane in plate 35 and Messalina in plate 45), all of which are antithetical to the notion of a virginally pure national emblem. Undermining such familiar symbols as the maritime trident and royal lion are the grotesques on the canopy, Britannia's dress and the French furnishings and pierrot costumes of Mr Punch and the dog. Such a Britannia cannot defend Britain's coastline any more than Beardsley's art grows out of British soil.

The prospect of social decay caused by the enfranchisement of 'deviant' subcultures and the incursions of 'outsiders' is something that continues to characterise certain discourses at the approach of our own *fin-de-siècle*. Many parallels might be drawn between the rhetoric of cultural crisis during the two periods. In the late twentieth century new computer technologies are challenging our dominant forms of cultural exchange, as the internet and other electronic media increasingly replace newspapers, periodicals and books. The question of who has access to ever-increasing amounts of information has led to renewed speculation about what constitutes notions of authenticity and authority. The increasing rights secured by gays and lesbians, women and racial minorities continue to stimulate intense controversies, while the moral panics surrounding such issues as affirmative action, AIDs, aboriginal rights, abortion, child abuse, religious fundamentalism, immigration, the national debt, political correctness, pornography and the welfare state only serve to exacerbate the growing sense of social polarisation. In some respects, recent controversies over Robert Mapplethorpe's work and threats to remove public funding from agencies that support such gay artists form a disconcerting echo to Harry Quilter's call for the public condemnation of Beardsley. As Elaine Showalter has emphasised in a recent exploration of *fin-de-siècle* anxieties:

> In periods of cultural insecurity, when there are fears of regression and degeneration, the longing for strict border controls around the definition of gender, as well as race, class, and nationality, becomes especially intense. If the different races can be kept in their places, if the various classes can be held in their proper districts of the city, and if men and women can be fixed in their separate spheres, many hope, apocalypse can be prevented and we can preserve a comforting sense of identity and permanence in the face of that relentless spectre of millennial change.[15]

The hopeful 'many', to whom Showalter refers, have more often than not, been associated with a neo-conservative return to traditional social values and structures predicated on fixed identities and a reaffirmation of timeless moral standards. Needless to say, this logic has been exposed by the post-structuralist critiques of a wide range of postmodernist thinkers who have drawn attention to the highly constructed and contingent nature of social systems. Interestingly for our purposes, the notion of theatricality has proven central for many postmodernist critiques, as Steven Connor elaborates:

> Any theatrical work exemplifies the tension between product and process, for a dramatic work can never exist fully either in its script version, or in any individual performance of that script. Any script must advertise its incompleteness, its necessity of being embodied in more than mere printed words, while any performance must always refer back to some notational script . . . This split is actualized in socio-economic forms as well. More than any other cultural form, the theatre encompasses the extremes of high and low culture; the radiant glory of 'classic drama' . . . and . . . the inescapable physical and commercial pressures on the theatre as a social and economic institution . . . Theatricality stands for all those falsifying divisions which complicate, diffuse and displace the concentrated self-identity of a work of art, and so encompasses a number of different effects, including self-consciousness of the spectator, the awareness of context and the dependence upon extension in time.[16]

By emphasising the performative nature of cultural and social systems, many postmodern critics have argued that concepts like morality, gender, or racial and social identity are created by social conventions whose rules vary according to who the participants are and the way they play the game, as well as their temporal and geographic location. For many writers, such thinking has enabled a radical critique of the social status quo since performances can be changed. For example, in feminist terms, Judith Butler has stressed that gender is performative rather than essentialist, noting that:

> acts, gestures and desires produce the effect of an internal core or substance, but produce this *on the surface of the body*, through the play of signifying absences that suggest but never reveal the organizing principle of identity as a cause. Such acts, gestures, enactments, generally construed, are *performative* in the sense that the essence or identity that they otherwise purport to express are *fabrications* manufactured and sustained through corporeal signs and other discursive means. That the gendered body is performative suggests that it has no ontological status apart from the various acts which constitute its reality.[17]

I would argue that it is this disturbing sense of performative bodies in fabricated worlds which many critics have found perverse, morbid and decadent in Beardsley's art. In addition to claiming that Beardsley's images were grotesque and evil, 'philistine' reviewers of the 1890s usually ended up concluding that his work was utterly eccentric and meaningless. As one writer discussing Beardsley's work in the first *Yellow Book* demanded, 'What does it mean? What is it for? What is the want which it is intended to supply? . . . Who wants these fantastic pictures like Japanese sketches gone mad . . . Who wants anything in the picture division of this black-and-yellow volume?'[18]

The charge that Beardsley's images refused to add up to anything recognisably coherent was reiterated by art writers such as Margaret Armour who angrily asserted:

> Mr Beardsley has a trick of superimposing one style on another – Japanese on medieval,

medieval on Celtic. That does not matter so long as he has the genius to unify; but what does matter is that the groundwork of them all should be Cockney, and the coster so prominent in the motifs.[19]

She went on to complain about this persistent mixing of styles which always ended up being disconcertingly *outré*, vulgar and working-class. Leaving aside Armour's charges of Cockney impudence, to which we will return later, it is important to stress that Beardsley's frequent stylistic shifts were a major source of irritation.

From the beginning of his professional artistic career in 1893 until his death in 1898, Beardsley experimented with different styles as he moved from one project to another. The medievalising tendencies of Beardsley's illustrations for Sir Thomas Malory's *Le Morte Darthur* (plates 24-28) were improvised playfully from the work of Edward Burne-Jones, William Morris and other Pre-Raphaelite artists. According to Beardsley's close friend, Aymer Vallance, Morris was infuriated by the fact that Beardsley so accurately and irreverently reproduced the essential elements of Morris's style. Apparently, had it not been for the intervention of Burne-Jones, Morris would have written a letter protesting such plagiarism to Beardsley's publisher, JM Dent.[20] The illustrations for Oscar Wilde's *Salomé* (plates 1-8), Beardsley's next important commission, were referred to by the artist as his 'Japonesques,' although they evidently did not appeal to Oscar Wilde, perhaps because the author was caricatured in several of the drawings (see, for example, plate 4: *The Eyes of Herod*). Evidently, Wilde felt that Beardsley had stylistically misrepresented the spirit of the play, remarking that 'I admire, I do not like Aubrey's illustrations. They are too Japanese, while my play is Byzantine.'[21] The following year, from 1894 to 1895, his work for the *Yellow Book* and other projects (plates 38, 41, 49) was largely inspired by contemporary graphic illustrators working in England and France such as Dudley Hardy and Jules Cheret, whose work and comments were published next to Beardsley's in an article entitled 'The Art of the Hoarding' in 1894.[22] By 1896, when Beardsley had started working almost exclusively for Leonard Smithers on projects such as the *Savoy* (plates 29-35, 57-59) and *The Rape of the Lock* (plates 14-19), he turned to neo-classical and rococo sources from the eighteenth-century, while in the *Lysistrata* illustrations of the same year (plates 11-13) the artist utilised designs from the decoration of Greek pottery.

It is important to stress that in each case the borrowed style simply provided a starting point for the artist's own experimentation; elements were reworked fantastically in addition to being recycled with others from different periods and places. A typical example of such eclectic embroidery is Beardsley's fifth illustration for *The Rape of the Lock* (plate 18) which depicts the Baron cutting off the lock of Belinda's hair. While the whole image evokes a rococo sensibility with its elaborately stippled surfaces and curvilinear floral garlands and patterns, certain details seem curiously out of place. As Brian Reade notes, while the style of the men's clothing is appropriate, that of the women's dates from the 1780s, some seventy years after the date of Pope's poem. Similarly, some of the furnishings (such as Belinda's carved Thonet chair) are equally anachronistic.[23] Chris Snodgrass further suggests that Beardsley deliberately emphasised a number of grotesque details, including the outline of Belinda's dress, which resembles erotically enlarged buttocks, and the phallus-shaped tendrils of her hair. Snodgrass also argues that Beardsley seems to have perversely enjoyed marginalising the central character of Belinda, who is partially cropped by the left edge of the frame, and foregrounding that of a dwarf drinking chocolate, who is not even in the poem.[24]

Beardsley certainly seems to have revelled in the imagination of such bizarre worlds. In a revealing (and comically inflated) letter to his friend GF Scotson-Clark, the artist explained how he and William Morris differed when it came to reviving medieval imagery: 'The truth is that, while his work is a mere imitation of the old stuff, mine is fresh and original.' Elsewhere in the letter he described drawing subjects which were 'quite mad and a little indecent. Strange hermaphroditic creatures wandering about in Pierrot costumes or modern dress; quite a new world of my own creation.' Summing up his achievements, Beardsley added that all of this work had far out-distanced the 'old black-and-white duffers.'[25] In this sense, then, Beardsley was something of an artistic performer trying on different styles at will as well as stretching the limits of their credibility. Such constant role-playing undermined the notion of a stable artistic identity or source of originality. For many critics of Beardsley's day, this constant playing with styles and conventions made it difficult to take his work seriously.

The assumption of different guises and roles was something which had fascinated Beardsley from a very early age. At Brighton Grammar School, which he attended until the age of sixteen, he was involved in staging numerous student performances, including a farce he wrote entitled *A Brown Study*, which was reviewed in the local newspapers. One of his contemporaries and fellow actors at the school was the future impresario, CB Cochran, whose career Beardsley traced with interest until the end of his life. Of even greater importance to him was the theatrical career of his beloved sister, Mabel, who became a professional actress after abandoning a brief stint of teaching. During their spare time after moving to London in 1888, Aubrey and Mabel had enthusiastically mounted amateur theatricals at what they called 'The Cambridge Theatre of Varieties' which referred to their home address of 32 Cambridge Street in Pimlico where the family resided in a lodging house during 1890. Brigid Brophy has suggested that these amateur events provided the subject for Beardsley's series of three drawings, *The Comedy Ballet of Marionettes*, published in the second *Yellow Book*.[26] In these illustrations the dramatic narrative of a lesbian courtship presided over by leering dwarfs was described ironically as being staged by 'The Troupe of the Theatre-Impossible.'

Beardsley's passion for dressing up and playing roles was recorded by friends as well as in his own letters. Henry Harland, who edited the *Yellow Book* with Beardsley, recalled:

> He loved a romp, a masquerade, a harmless practical joke. One evening I was seated in my study, when the servant brought a visiting-card, on which was written 'Miss Tibbett and Master Tibbett.' I went into the drawing room, and there was Miss Beardsley with a tall boy in an Eton jacket. The tall boy in the Eton jacket — Master Tibbett, if you please — was Aubrey, jubilant, laughing for delight in his own prank.[27]

In this reminiscence published several months after Beardsley's death, Harland stresses with fondness the schoolboy innocence of the artist's sartorial games. During his own lifetime, however, Beardsley tended to emphasise the more disturbing implications of dressing-up. For instance, in a letter written in September of 1893 to his publisher John Lane, Beardsley commented, 'I am going to Jimmie's on Thursday night dressed up as a tart and mean to have a regular spree.'[28] Jimmie's was a reference to the St James Restaurant in Picadilly, a well known venue of prostitution and other illicit activities.

In addition to staging their own performances, Beardsley and his sister were avid theatre-goers. His letters referred frequently to the latest performances of Shakespeare, Wagner, Ibsen and numerous modern plays of the season. He avidly followed those performers he particularly admired, such as Ellen Terry, Sarah Bernhardt, Mrs Patrick Campbell, Réjane (plate 35) and Winnifred Emery, all of whom appeared in various sketches and drawings which were published in the periodical press.[29] Between 1893 and 1894 Beardsley became publicly associated with the cause of the 'new theatre,' first by illustrating Oscar Wilde's *Salomé* (plates 1-8), one of the most scandalous plays of the period, and then by designing a poster for Florence Farr's season of experimental plays at the Avenue Theatre. In the case of *Salomé*, Beardsley achieved notoriety not only because his 'Japonesque' style of illustration struck the public as unprecedented but also because the play had been refused a licence in 1892 on the grounds that Biblical characters could not be represented on the English stage.[30] This infamous decision, which stopped a production starring Sarah Bernhardt in the title role, made the play scandalous long before Beardsley illustrated it for John Lane in 1894.[31] In the second instance, Beardsley's association with Farr, the actress-manageress of the Avenue Theatre, was almost as *risqué* given that she produced plays by John Toddhunter, George Bernard Shaw and other advanced playwrights who, in her words, 'no ordinary management would take up.'[32] Beardsley's controversial blue and green poster of a woman standing behind a spotted curtain immediately attracted attention and was widely discussed and caricatured in the press.[33]

The artist evidently relished media attention, occasionally sending public 'letters to the editor' defending his work. After encountering one rather venomous review by Haldane Macfall, Beardsley wrote to the editor of *St Paul's*:

Sir,

No one more than myself welcomes frank, nay hostile, criticism, or enjoys more thoroughly a personal remark. But your art critic surely goes a little too far in last week's issue of *St Paul's*, and I may be forgiven if I take up the pen of resentment. He says that I am 'sexless and unclean'. As to my uncleanliness, I do the best for it in my morning bath, and if he has really any doubts as to my sex, he may come and see me take it.

Yours etc, Aubrey Beardsley[34]

Although he was finally persuaded to withdraw the letter, its tone indicates how much Beardsley enjoyed teasing his critics and testing the publicly defined limits of acceptable morality. In another instance the artist humorously countered moral reformers' objections to the costumes of female ballet dancers whose exposed limbs were watched voyeuristically by male music-hall-goers. In 1894 Mrs Ormiston Chant, a leading member of the National Vigilance Association and chief organiser of the infamous crusade against the Empire Theatre, claimed that she could easily design a more decent dancing costume. Beardsley could not resist provocatively offering his own solution to the problem in a drawing originally titled *A Suggested Reform in Ballet Costume* (plate 46). Here, by decoratively wrapping the woman from head to toe, Beardsley's drawing carries the reformers' plans to absurd lengths.

It should be stressed that such performative antics both in the press and in letters to his publishers and friends often compensated for activities the increasingly ill artist was unable to realise in everyday life. The lively and amusing correspondent was frequently confined to bed with acutely haemorrhaging lungs. From an early age, Beardsley was aware that his tuberculosis placed severe limitations on his time and energy, both of which he protected zealously. For Beardsley, life was lived most fully and satisfyingly in a world of books, drawings, music, theatre and letters. His cultural breadth astonished many contemporaries, including Arthur Symons who remarked that Beardsley, 'seemed to have read everything, and had his preferences as adroitly in order, as wittily in evidence, as almost any man of letters; indeed, he seemed to know more, and was a sounder critic, of books than of pictures; with perhaps a deeper feeling for music than for either.'[35] Because the cultural sphere offered a compensatory world for Beardsley, his endless erotic joking and celebration of polymorphously perverse pleasures was rather complicated, as Karl Beckson explains:

> Seizing upon the nineteenth-century obsession with the idea of artist as priest, Beardsley methodically enacted the role as his wish to transform his vulnerable body into enduring art. With wit and verve, he focused upon the phallus as the visible symbol of redemption, although he also saw its comic and shocking potentialities as well. Within the world of the imagination, autonomous and transcendent, Beardsley played out his drama of desperation while his body followed an inevitable course of decay.[36]

Although explicit depictions of the theatre formed a relatively minor part of Beardsley's oeuvre, many of his other drawings utilised theatrical conventions. Artificial bodies are carefully arranged in equally stylised settings. The lighting is seldom natural. For example, the fifth illustration of Pope's *Rape of the Lock* (1896) (plate 17) seems to take place in a theatre box, at least judging from the evening dress and fan and the architectural setting. It is only upon scrutinising the marginal details of the trees and water in the upper right and the oar in the lower left that one realises the characters are actually sitting on a barge. Another curiously theatrical spectacle is ostensibly mounted on the keys of a piano in Beardsley's drawing for the front cover of the advertising prospectus for the *Savoy* (plate 32). Here, a large John Bull appears on stage between the curtain and footlights bearing a prospectus announcing the forthcoming performance. As Brian Reade notes, Beardsley's original design (we see the expurgated version here) offended certain contributors to the magazine, including George Moore, who asked the publisher, Leonard Smithers, to withdraw it because Beardsley had irreverently portrayed John Bull with a diminutive erection. Apparently Smithers readily agreed since all of the copies had already been circulated.[37] Linda Zatlin further suggests that the juxtaposition of John Bull and the child peeking out under the curtain was intended to represent the contrast between established artists and the new artists whose work would appear in the *Savoy*. John Bull, a bloated creature, lacks the child's knowledge of what goes on behind the curtain or in the pages of the magazine.[38] The title page for the first issue of the *Savoy* (plate 33) continued such theatrical allusions by presenting two costumed masqueraders standing in a highly contrived interior which is evoked by a small number of carefully placed objects including two large billowing curtains.

Other similarly theatrical conventions include the dramatic black-and-white contrasts, spotlighting, and costumes that are used in his illustration of Messalina from the sixth satire of Juvenal (plate 45) and in a drawing entitled *The Scarlet Pastorale* (plate 50) which was first published in the *Sketch* and later in *The London Year Book*. The latter seems to have been an imaginary theatrical performance much like his earlier series, *The Comedy Ballet of Marionettes*. Here, Beardsley used *commedia dell'arte* characters such as the diamond-patterned harlequin in the foreground. (The *commedia dell'arte* figure of pierrot – which can be seen in plates 29, 31, 33, and 38 – was probably Beardsley's favourite.[39]) In this drawing Beardsley deliberately emphasised the unnatural by making the masqueraders on the backcloth seem as real as the harlequin. Again, the carefully choreographed arrangement of figures underlines the fact that this is not a scene from everyday life.

It should be emphasised that theatrical artifice is only one of Beardsley's defamiliarising strategies, which also included anachronistic mixing of styles and periods, displaced narrative focal points, grotesque exaggeration and a bizarre use of framing and cropping. Many of these strategies have been explored recently in deconstructive readings of Beardsley's art. For instance, working within a Derridean critical paradigm, Chris Snodgrass demonstrates that Beardsley's aesthetic involved cultural caricature and endlessly 'oscillating' meanings. In an intriguing analysis of the artist's illustration *La Beale Isoud at Joyous Gard* for *Le Morte Darthur* (plate 27) Snodgrass analyses the constant confusion between the categories of nature and artifice. What initially seems like an image of a demure woman in a natural setting is soon undermined by an erotically-charged frame of decorative pears which have 'strategically placed indentations, protuberances and dots' that resemble grotesquely misaligned breasts. The dots on the pears also double as voyeuristic eyes that draw attention to what is initially hidden in the interior picture. There, the artificial quality of the landscape is underlined by foreground trees whose branches are attached with cords and also by the mysterious white band behind the distant trees which could be either a natural river or else a man-made wall. The figure of Isoud seems less innocent when one considers that her breasts resemble the pears of the frame, her cloak is decorated with 'peacock eyes' or holes and the position of her hand makes it look as if she could pluck one of the surrounding phallic trees. Here we witness an erosion of the conventional boundaries separating virginal innocence and erotic knowledge, nature and artifice, as well as those of picture and frame.

According to Snodgrass, such visual jokes were part of a deliberately elitist and highly convenient strategy of catering to a 'perceptive elite' who got the joke that 'philistine 'outsiders' missed:

> For Beardsley, Decadent elitism, which dictated that brilliance should not be wholly accessible to the vulgar masses, converged nicely with bourgeois prudery, which demanded that the salacious elements of life be kept out of sight or disguised as respectable.[40]

Snodgrass concludes by stressing that Beardsley's stylistic defamiliarisations 'were a strategy to salvage transcendental truth by positing the ultimate authority of Art – style untrammelled by preclusive meanings.' But from Snodgrasss's Derridean perspective, even Beardsley's limited truth claim for art fails as it too inevitably succumbs to the general crisis of meaning created by the endless play of difference. Instead, one realises that all logocentric texts are 'fictions whose meaning oscillates, subject to and at the mercy of manipulations that are no more the final word than the "sources" they refashion.'[41] Beardsley's modernity consists of relentlessly drawing our attention to this fact.

While such deconstructive accounts have yielded fascinating insights into the formal structure of the artist's work, they have also tended to lose sight of what was at stake for Beardsley's various constituencies of viewers at particular historical moments. In other words, who were the perceptive insiders and philistine outsiders that Snodgrass describes so suggestively? And what happened when they encountered Beardsley's imagery? After all, people like the actress, Florence Farr, and the publishers, John Lane and Leonard Smithers, deliberately commissioned Beardsley's work because they thought it represented something that would attract their target audiences, in the same way that critics like Harry Quilter could identify what they disliked. At least part of what seems to have been radically disruptive and daringly modern about Beardsley's imagery was its new hybrid visual language that combined quotations from 'high' literary and artistic masterpieces with all sorts of 'low' references to popular and mass cultural forms.

We can trace some of these elements in Beardsley's illustration, *Lucian's Strange Creatures* (plate 22) which was intended for but rejected from Lawrence and Bullen's 1894 edition of *Lucian's True History*. Once again we see Beardsley utilising the highly stylised conventions and flat perspectives of contemporary posters. Included in the illustration are a mixed cast of characters and references which encompass pagan mythology in the figure of the satyr, Christianity in the case of the snake, Japonisme in the central figure on the far left, English aestheticism represented by Whistler's butterfly in the upper left, pornography and guise in the shape of a masked pierrot fondling a woman in the centre, and contemporary popular satire which probably inspired Beardsley's tall, darkly-dressed woman in the centre, who seems to be based on cartoon images of the stereotypical 'New Woman' of the nineties. Linda Zatlin has recently suggested that the image was refused for publication because it confronted the traditional compartmentalisation of femininity by emphasising the relationship between sexual activity and motherhood without turning the women into passive erotic objects:

> Because the woman so lightly holds the frowning baby or foetus – whose pointed finger perhaps accuses her of aborting it – this female seems to ready herself to thrust motherhood away from her so that she may partake of the sexual revels enjoyed by the couple at her side and encouraged by the grinning faces and sly snake . . . Yet examined without the 1890s bias against works which could be interpreted as sexually and therefore immorally suggestive, Beardsley's drawing reveals, even urges, the close connection between sexuality and motherhood. The snake and the satyr, the knowing faces push the couple and the mother close together in the composition as if acknowledging motherhood

as a result of sexual play. Such a reading explains the satyr's quizzical look at the Wildean (homosexual) profile and the woman's insistent stare which, coupled with the proffered baby (who may be reaching out towards its mother), demands recognition of her status as a mother.[42]

Although Zatlin's interpretation explains why a 'New Woman' actress-manageress and feminist like Florence Farr admired Beardsley's work as well as why he was chosen to illustrate John Lane's socially critical Keynotes series of 'new' writers, it does not help us understand why the image was first published in 1906 by Leonard Smithers, a speciality publisher and bookseller of limited editions, who made much of his money selling erotica and pornography. While it might be argued that all sexually explicit imagery was potentially titillating during this period, Smithers was especially interested in Beardsley's work which he continued to commission until the end of the artist's life, often sending money he could ill afford.[43] Such diverse patterns of patronage indicate that various sectors of Beardsley's public appreciated his work for different reasons that still await detailed study. While we still need to know more about how Beardsley's work was consumed by different viewers, it is evident that his supporters believed that the artist's new hybrid aesthetic somehow addressed their own unstable and largely marginal status as modern avant-garde artists and writers, emancipated new women, homosexuals or variously 'deviant' subcultural figures.

The fact that Beardsley's style embodied a number of disturbing new challenges was something 'philistine outsiders' like Margaret Armour and Harry Quilter recognised and persistently equated with 'Cockney' impudence and vulgarity. Such charges also appeared in a cartoon entitled *How It Is Done (An Art-Recipe.)* (fig 4) published in an 1894 issue of *Punch,* which shows a decadent dandy in evening dress flirting with a woman who initially looks like an 'East-End Arriet' or prostitute with the coarse facial features and fashions (note the large ornately decorated hat and gaudy dress) that characterised cartoon stereotypes of such women during the period.[44] The juxtaposition of black and white expanses, the use of dotted patterns as well as the grotesque details of the insects and skull left no doubt who was being targeted. In case viewers missed the point, under the cartoonist's signature in the upper left corner was inscribed 'with apologies to', followed by Beardsley's distinctive mark. Looking at the image more closely and reading the accompanying poem reveals that Beardsley's art was represented as some sort of music-hall performance. The fact that the two figures are on stage is indicated by the dotted curtain behind them. The poem develops this idea by suggesting that Beardsley's new style of art involves making a figure like 'front-row Tottie' pose with a hat as worn by 'Coster Loo'. The scene itself is described as looking like 'a slum in foggy weather'.

Evidently such critics feared the emergence of a modern cultural form that was both popular and critical at the same time; that could reach large audiences and make them consider overturning all sorts of conventions by demanding a more imaginative and pleasurable life. Brigid Brophy points to the particularly modern threat that Beardsley's easily reproducible art posed:

His work acknowledged that for modern people pictures are not things that you hang on the wall of your country house and absorb by leisured connoisseurship. They are things you look at reproduced in books . . . Having worked all day, you look at the pictures in books by artificial light. The most modern thing about Beardsley was that he drew by the same type of light as his drawings would be seen by.[45]

Conservative critics do not seem to have been troubled by the elitism of Beardsley's art; what was much more frightening was its democratic potential. What would happen if increasing numbers of male and female readers from the lower classes embraced this kind of art? By equating Beardsley's performative aesthetic with vulgar forms of music-hall entertainment, conservative critics attempted to ward off the likelihood of this happening. After all, most upwardly mobile book-purchasing members of the lower classes would hardly want to be identified with the coster, the Cockney and the music-hall, since those were precisely the sorts of cultural stereotypes they wanted to leave behind. It was a theme 'philistine' critics returned to time and again when reviewing Beardsley's work. Condemning not only the art of Beardsley but also that of P Wilson Steer and Walter Sickert – whose reproductions appeared together in the third *Yellow Book* – an anonymous *Spectator* reviewer summed things up by complaining: 'There is a curious air of unreality, an artificial, theatrical, music-hall atmosphere about their productions, the work apparently of the left wing of the English impressionist school.'[46] It is thus apparent that there was a dangerous underside to Beardsley's performative aesthetic, one which the artist once revealingly described as a form of 'decorative realism.'[47]

Notes

1 Max Beerbohm, *The Works of Max Beerbohm*, Charles Scribner's Sons, New York, 1896, p160. Osbert Burdett laterrecycled the phrase in his study of Victorian decadence, see his *The Beardsley Period: An Essay in Perspective*, John Lane, The Bodley Head, London, 1925.

2 See the letter from Aubrey Beardsley to Leonard Smithers published in Henry Maas, JL Duncan and WG Good (eds), *The Letters of Aubrey Beardsley*, Cassell & Company, London, 1970, p132. Yvette Guilbert would have already been familiar toreaders of *To-Day* since an article by Stanley Clark had introduced her as the 'greatest café chantant singer in the world today', and included a photograph of her wearing long black gloves, see *To-Day*, May 12, 1894, p13.

3 *To-Day*, May 12, 1894, p28. The drawing was a caricature of Whistler's wife, Beatrice Godwin Whistler (Trixie), which Beardsley initially gave to William Rothenstein who later returned it urging the artist to destroy it. Beardsley had wanted the drawing published in the first *Yellow Book* and pleaded with his publisher, John Lane, to include it with the provocative title, *A Study in Major Lines* which openly parodied Whistler's own practice of entitling his works. Needless to say, Lane refused to publish the drawing.

4 Beardsley describes and illustrates what he calls his 'trademark' in a letter to his friend, GF Scotson-Clark dated cFebruary15, 1893, *Letters*, Maas et al (eds), p45.

5 Arthur Symons, 'The Decadent Movement in Literature', *Harper's New Monthly Magazine* 87, November 1893, pp858-67.

6 Arthur Symons, 'Aubrey Beardsley', *Fortnightly Review* no 63, May 1898, p755.

7 Ibid, pp754-55.

8 For a useful description of the 'process' technique, see Joseph Pennell, *Modern Illustration*, George Bell & Sons, London,1895, p42.

9 Rodney Shewan, 'Love Death, and Criticism: Three of Beardsley's Culs-de-lampe,' in Robert Langenfeld (ed), *Reconsidering Aubrey Beardsley*, UMI Research Press and Ann Arbor, 1989, p131.

10 The first volume of *Yellow Book* edited by Henry Harland and Aubrey Beardsley and published by John Lane of the Bodley Head appeared in April of 1894, the same month that George Bernard Shaw's *Arms and the Man* premiered. Florence Farr, the actress-manageress who first produced and starred in Shaw's play had commissioned a poster from Beardsley advertising her performance in *A Comedy of Sighs* also at the Avenue Theatre in March 1894.

11 Cited in Karl Beckson, *London in the 1890s: A Cultural History*, WW Norton and Company, New York, 1992, pxiv. Beckson provides an informative discussion of many of the 'new cultural forms of the period with chapters on 'The New Woman' and 'The New Drama', Also useful are John Stokes, *In the Nineties*, University of Chicago Press, Chicago, 1989 and his collection of edited essays *Fin de Siècle/Fin du Globe: Fears and Fantasies of the Late Nineteenth Century*, Macmillan, London, 1992.

12 On women's educational deficiencies during this period, see Janet E Hogarth, 'Literary Degenerates', *Fortnightly Review* no 57,1895, pp586-92. Some interesting recent discussions of 'New Women' writers include Linda Dowling, 'The Decadent and

the New Woman in the 1890s', *19th Century Fiction* 33, March 1979, pp434-453 and Penny Boumelha, Thomas Hardy and Women, Harvester Press, Brighton, 1982, ch 4 'Women and the New Fiction 1880-1900'.

13 Harry Quilter, 'The Gospel of Intensity,' *Contemporary Review* 67, June 1895, p781.

14 Ibid, p778.

15 Elaine Showalter, *Sexual Anarchy: Gender and Culture at the Fin de Siècle*, Viking, New York: 1990, p4.

16 Steven Connor, *Postmodernist Culture: An Introduction to the Contemporary*, Basil Blackwell, Oxford, 1989, p133.

17 Judith Butler, *Gender Trouble: Feminism and the Subversion of Identity*, Routledge, London, 1990, p136.

18 'Pages in Waiting', *World*, April 25, 1894 p21. For other similar charges, see also reviews from the *Academy*, April 28, 1894, p349 and the *Figaro*, April 19, 1894, p17.

19 Margaret Armour, 'Aubrey Beardsley and the Decadents', *Magazine of Art* 20, 1896, p10.

20 Aymer Vallance, 'The Invention of Aubrey Beardsley', *Magazine of Art* 22, 1898, pp363-64. Vallance states that after he showed Morris Beardsley's illustrations, Morris informed him that 'A man ought to do his own work.'

21 Sir William Rothenstein, *Men and Memories*, Faber & Faber, London, 1931, Vol 1 p184.

22 'The Art of the Hoarding', *New Review* 11, July 1894, pp47-55. He was, of course interested in the work of numerous other illustrators such as Toulouse-Lautrec, Grassette and Willet.

23 Brian Reade, *Aubrey Beardsley*, Bonanza Books, New York, 1967, p353.

24 Chris Snodgrass, 'Decadent Parodies: Aubrey Beardsley's Caricature of Meaning', in John Stokes (ed), *Fin de Siècle/Fin du Globe*, p201.

25 Beardsley also acknowledged that his work had greatly offended Morris, see Maas et al (eds), *Letters*, pp43-5. At the beginning of the same letter Beardsley discussed his similar reworking of Japanese sources by explaining his 'entirely new method of drawing and composition' was 'suggestive of Japan, but not really japonesque.' Elsewhere he describes his work as being in a 'mystico-Oriental' style, see *Letters*, p50.

26 Brigid Brophy, *Beardsley and His World*, Thames And Hudson, London, 1976, p41.

27 Henry Harland, 'Aubrey Beardsley', *Academy*, December 10, 1898, p437.

28 Maas et al (eds), *Letters*, p53.

29 Further discussions of Beardsley's theatrical work can be found in BJ Elliott, 'New and Not So New Women on the London Stage: Aubrey Beardsley's Yellow Book Images of Mrs Patrick Campbell and Réjane', *Victorian Studies*, Autumn 1987, pp33-57; BJ Elliott, 'Sights of Pleasure: Beardsley's Images of Actresses and the New Journalism of the Nineties', in Langenfeld (ed), *Reconsidering Aubrey Beardsley*, pp69-101, and John Stokes, 'Beardsley/Jarry: The Art of Deformation', in Langenfeld (ed), *Reconsidering Aubrey Beardsley*, pp54-69.

30 This event is discussed at some length in John Russell Stephens, *The Censorship of English Drama 1824-1901*, Cambridge University Press, Cambridge, 1980, ch 8, 'Moral Decorum and the Advancement of Drama'.

31 The question of whether the illustrations complemented, parodied or undermined the text has been widely debated and is too complicated to investigate here. For some useful recent discussions of the issue, see Ian Fletcher, Aubrey Beardsley, Twayne Publishers, Boston, 1987, ch 5 'Salomé'; Elliott L Gilbert, 'Tumult of Images: Wilde, Beardsley and Salomé', *Victorian Studies* 26, Winter 1983, pp133-59; and Jeffrey Wallen, 'Illustrating Salomé: perverting the text?' *Word & Image* 8:2, April-June 1992, pp124-32.

32 'The Comedy of Sighs', Theatre, May 1, 1894, p281.

33 The poster is reproduced in Reade, *Beardsley*, no 297, p319. For examples of the way the poster was reproduced in press, see an interview with Farr in the *Sketch*, March 28, 1894, p445 and a cartoon of the poster in *Punch*, April 21, 1894, p189.

34 Maas et al (eds), *Letters*, p92. For another such letter which was published, see the *Pall Mall Budget*, May 3, 1894, p20. In this case Beardsley defended himself against the charge of decadence in relation to his frontispiece for the first *Yellow Book* which depicted a woman playing a piano in an open field. Beardsley claimed the scene had been inspired by an actual event from the life of the composer, Gluck, whom no-one considered decadent.

35 Symons, 'Aubrey Beardsley', p752.

36 Karl Beckson, 'The Artist as Transcendent Phallus: Aubrey Beardsley and the Ritual of Defense,' in Langenfeld (ed), *Reconsidering Aubrey Beardsley*, p207.

37 Reade, *Beardsley*, p354. Reade reproduces the version with the offensive erection, see his plate 414.

38 Linda Gertner Zatlin, *Aubrey Beardsley and Victorian Sexual Politics*, Clarendon Press, Oxford, 1990, pp42-3.

39 For further discussions of the significance of the pierrot in Beardsley's art, see Milly Heyd, *Aubrey Beardsley: Symbol, Mask and Self-Irony*, Peter Lang, New York, 1986 and Chris Snodgrass, 'Beardsley's Oscillating Spaces: Play, Paradox, and the Grotesque,' in Langenfeld (ed), *Reconsidering Aubrey Beardsley*, pp19-52.

40 Snodgrass, 'Decadent Parodies,' p181.

41 Ibid, p206.

42 Zatlin, Beardsley, pp33-34.

43 For more information on Smithers's activities as a publisher, consult the introduction to RA Walker, (ed), *Letters from Aubrey Beardsley to Leonard Smithers*, First Edition Club, London, 1937, ppv-xvi and George Sims, 'Leonard Smithers: A Publisher of the Nineties,' *London Magazine* 3, September 1956, pp32-40.

44 See for example Leonard Raven-Hill and Phil May's numerous cartoons of Cockney and coster life which were widely published in special folios and throughout the periodical press during the nineties.

45 Brigid Brophy, *Black and White: A Portrait of Aubrey Beardsley*, Jonathan Cape, London, 1968, pp73, 76.

46 'The Yellow Book,' *Spectator*, November 17, 1894, p700.

47 Maas et al, (eds), *Letters*, p72.

The Plates

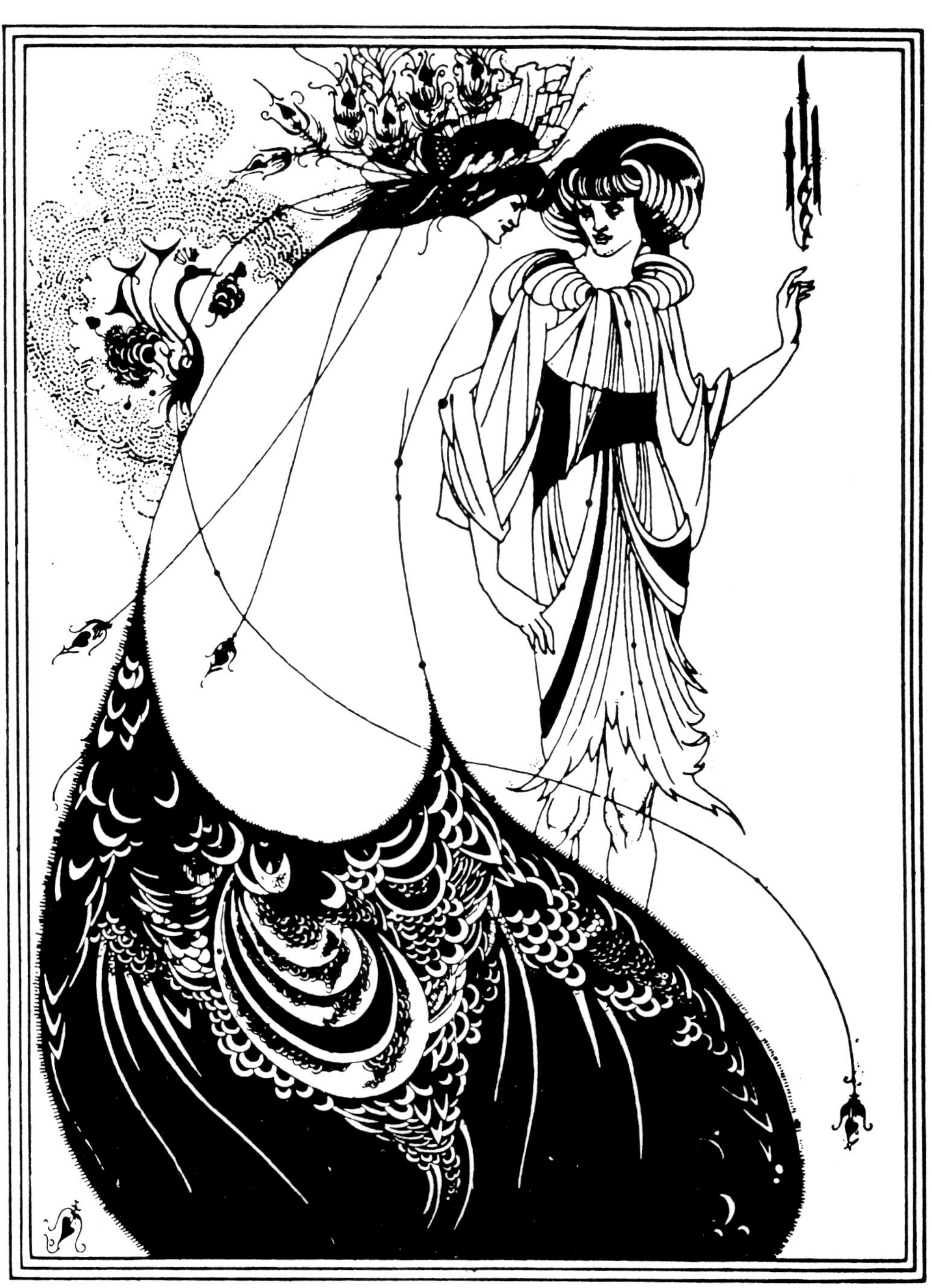

1

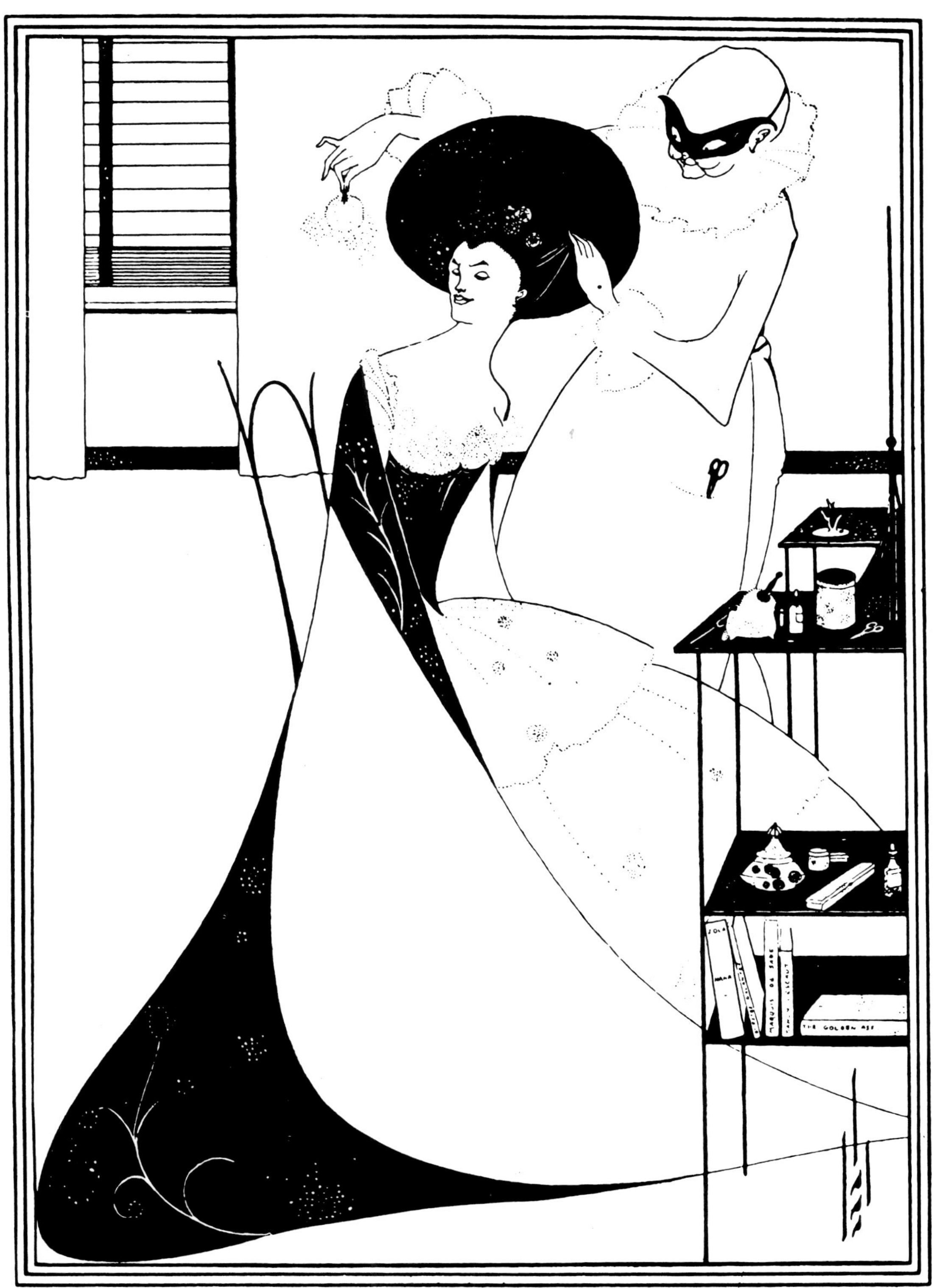

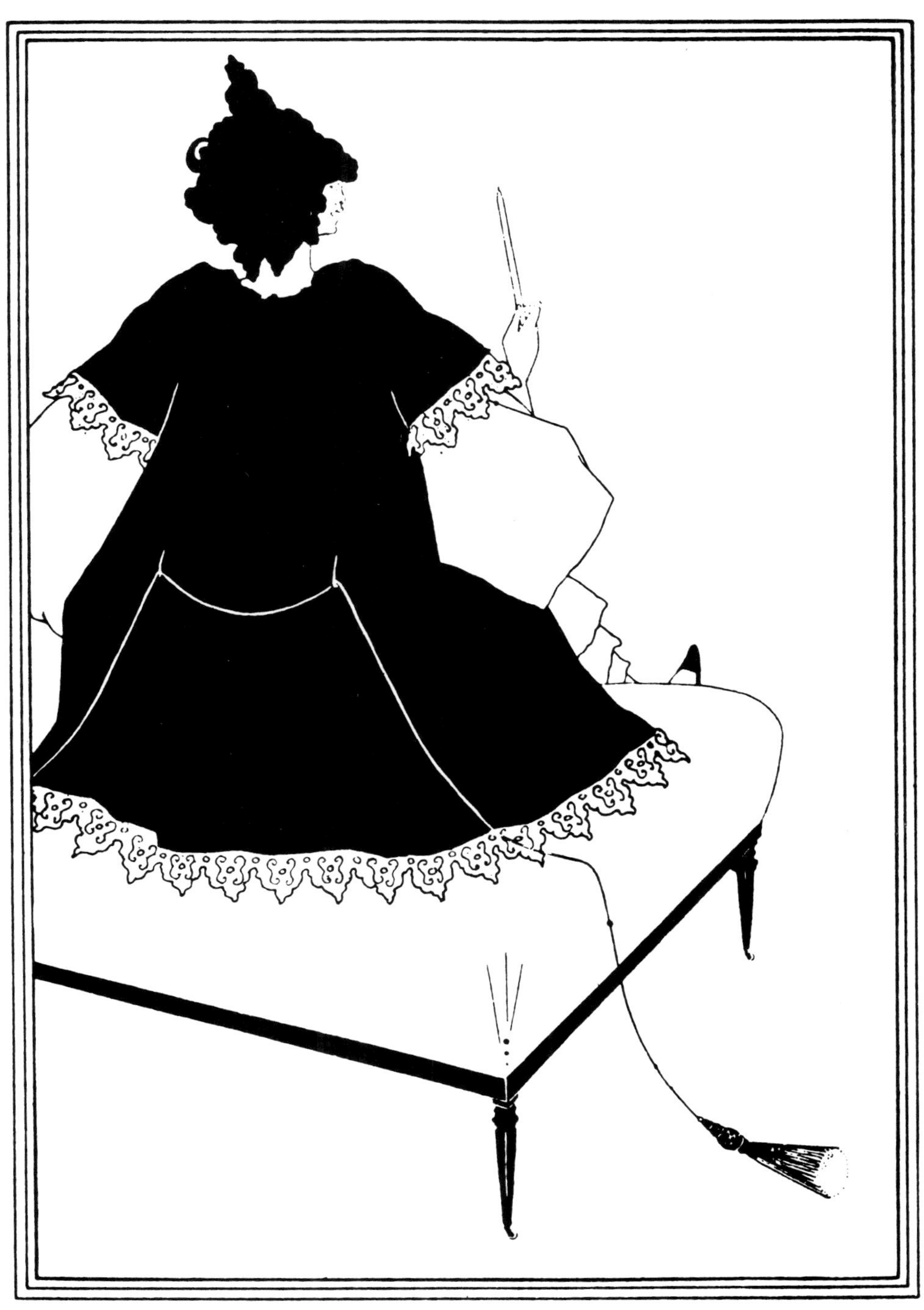

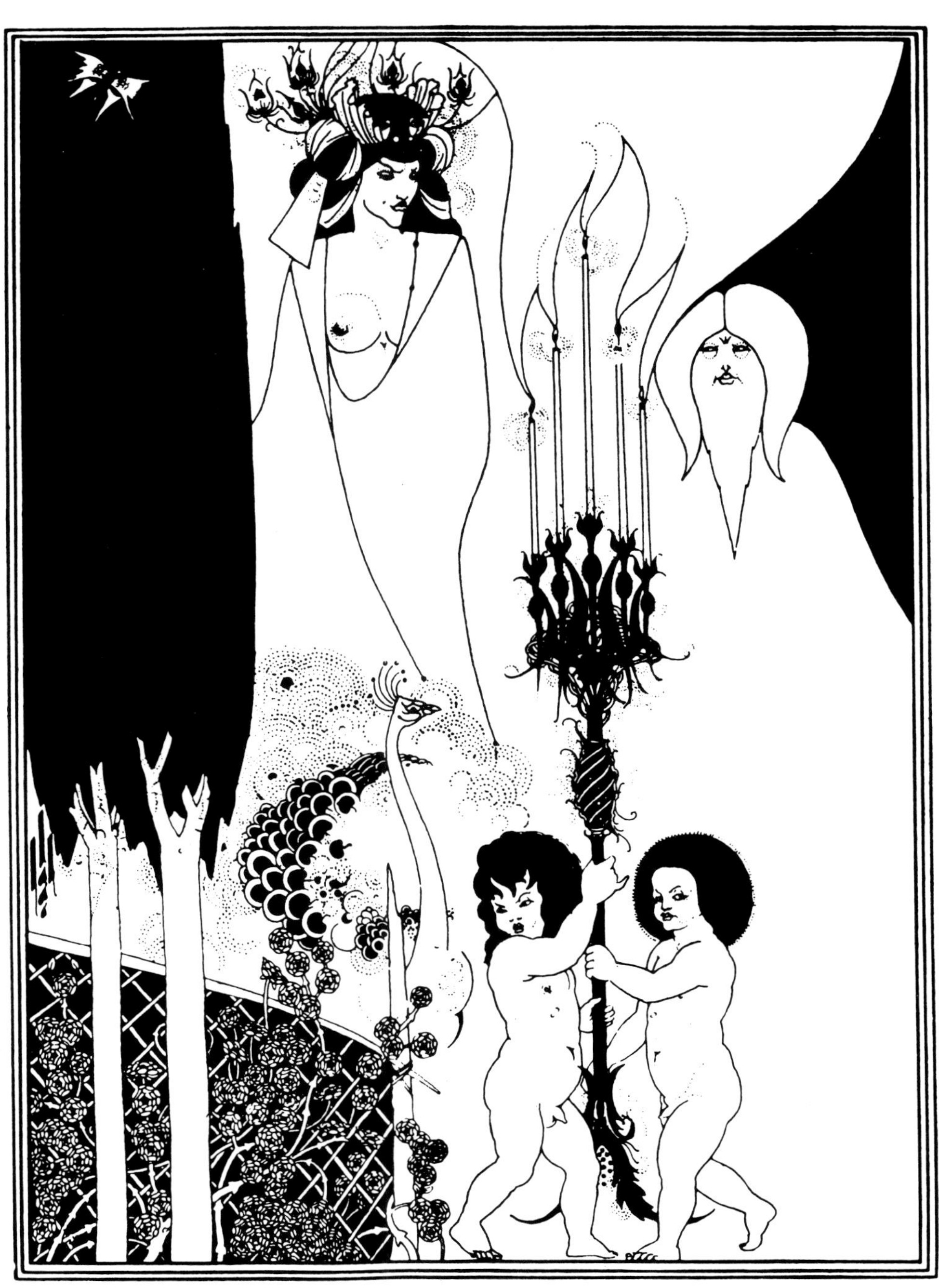

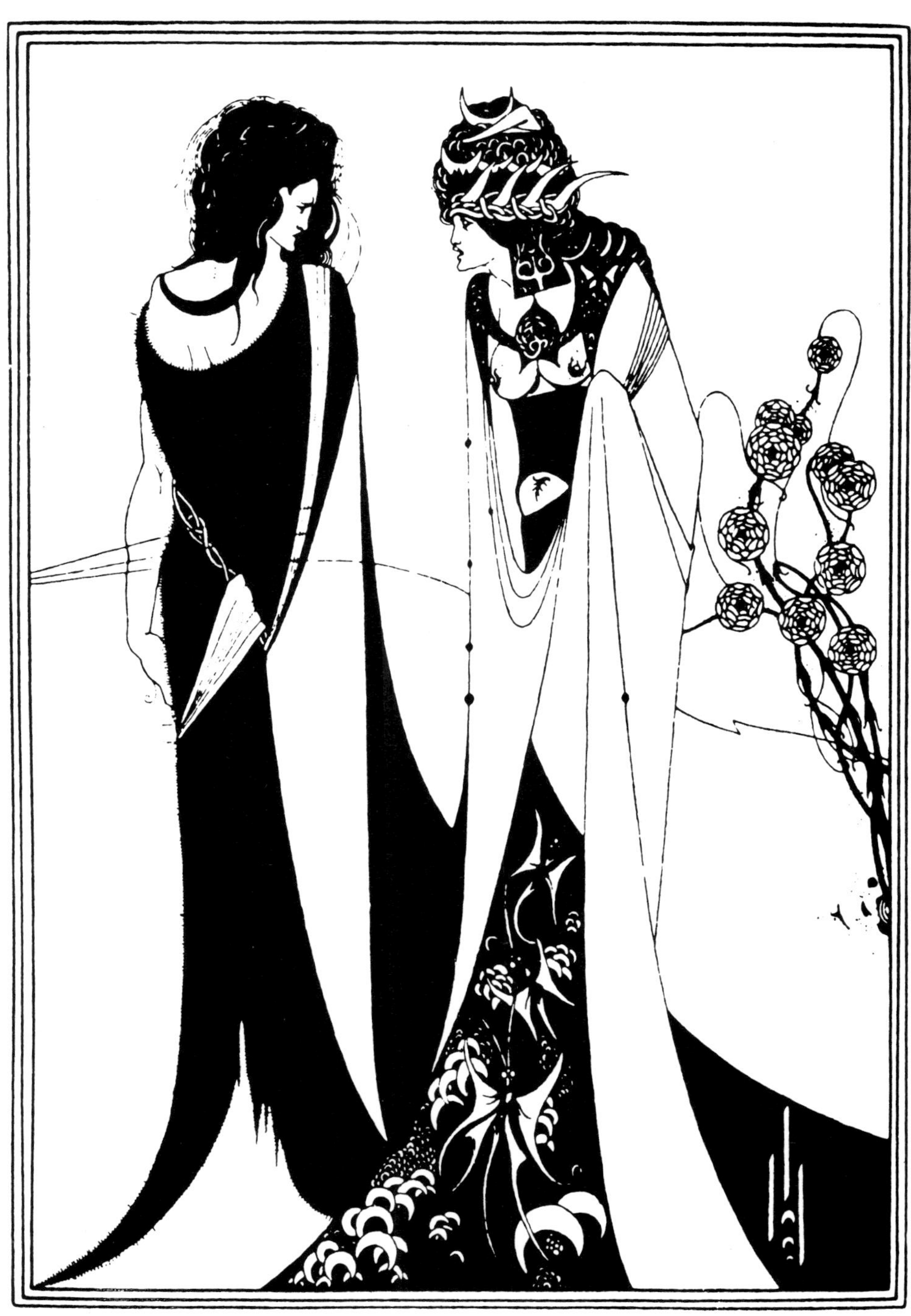

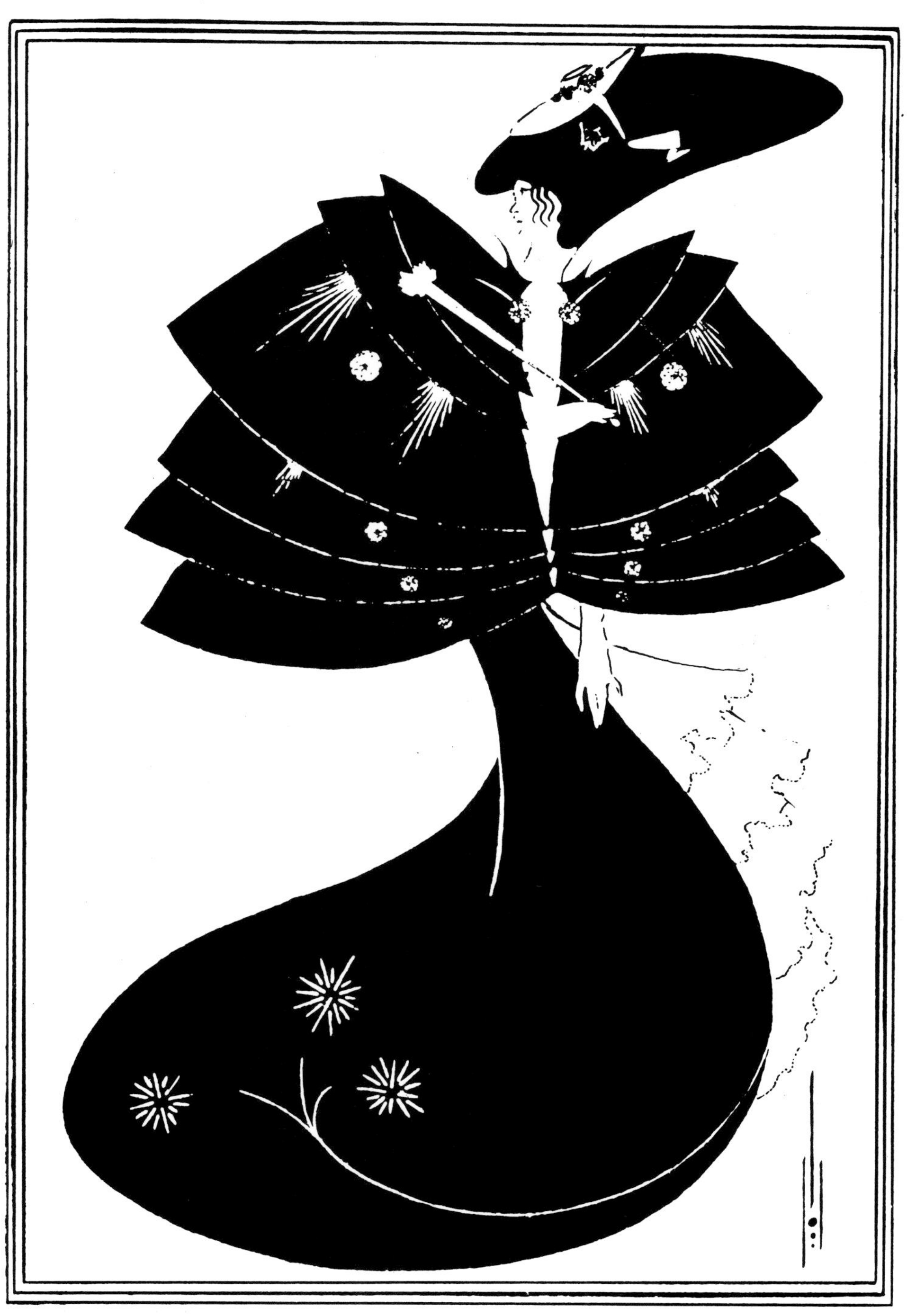

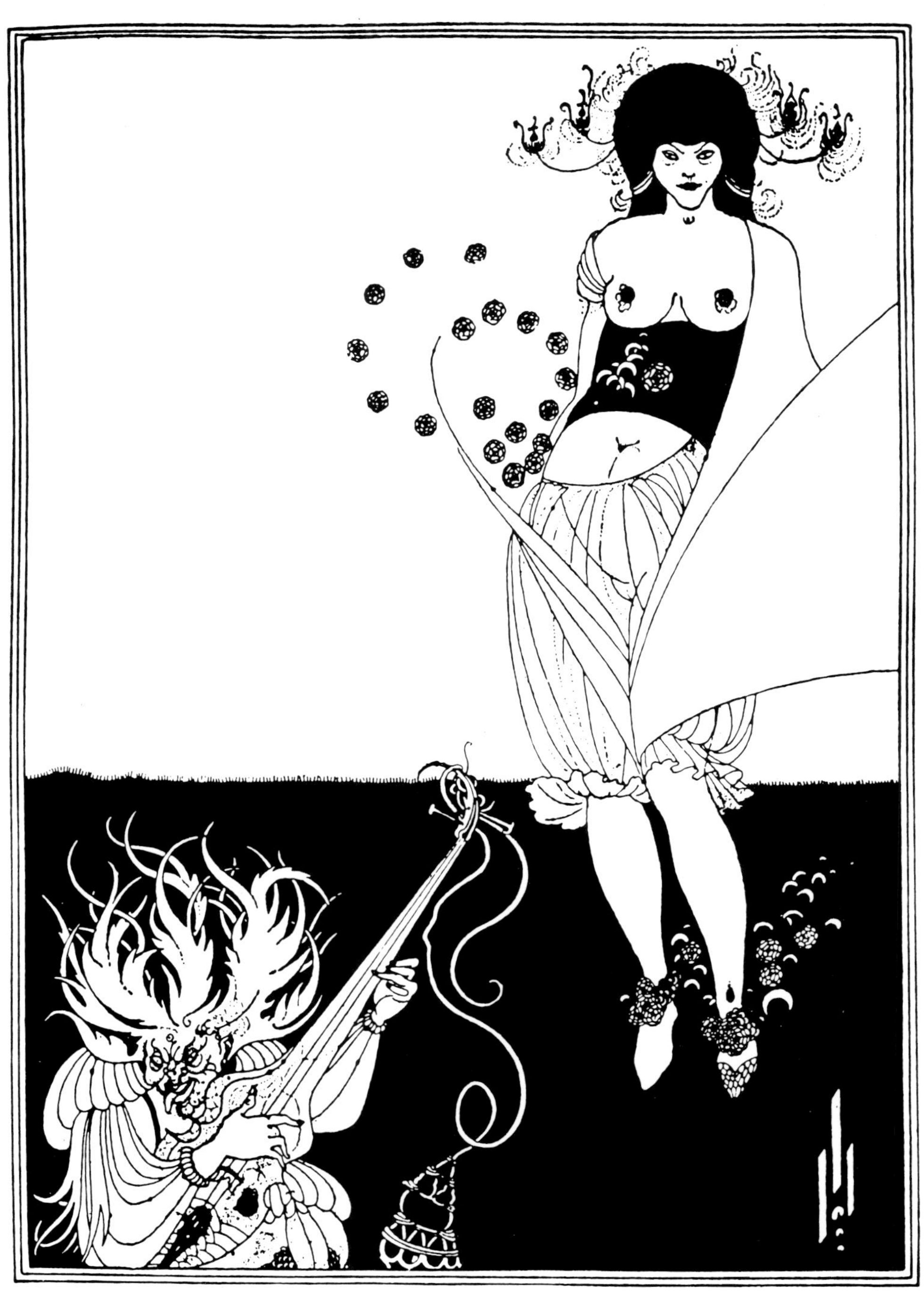

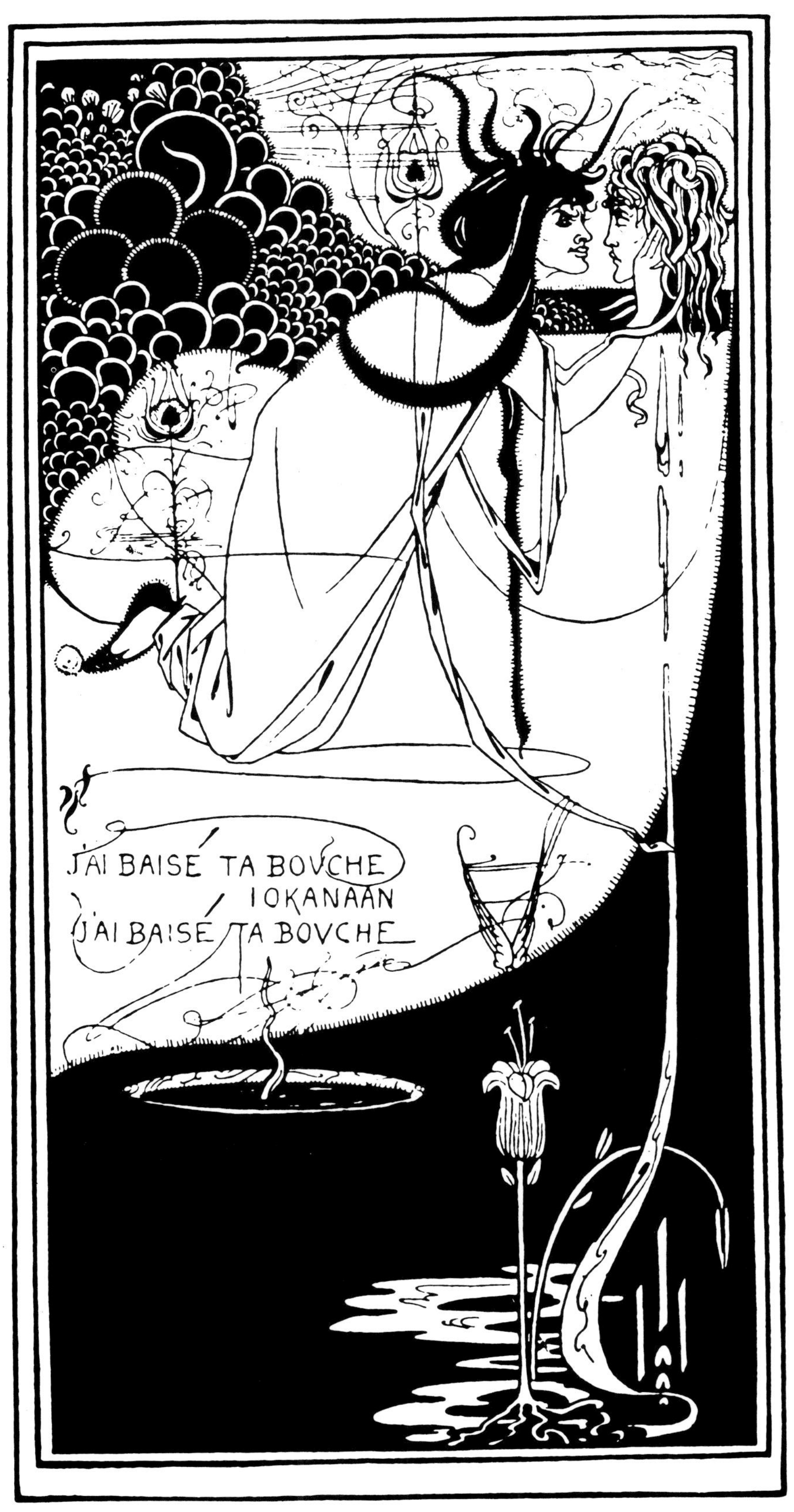

J'AI BAISÉ TA BOVCHE
IOKANAAN
J'AI BAISÉ TA BOVCHE

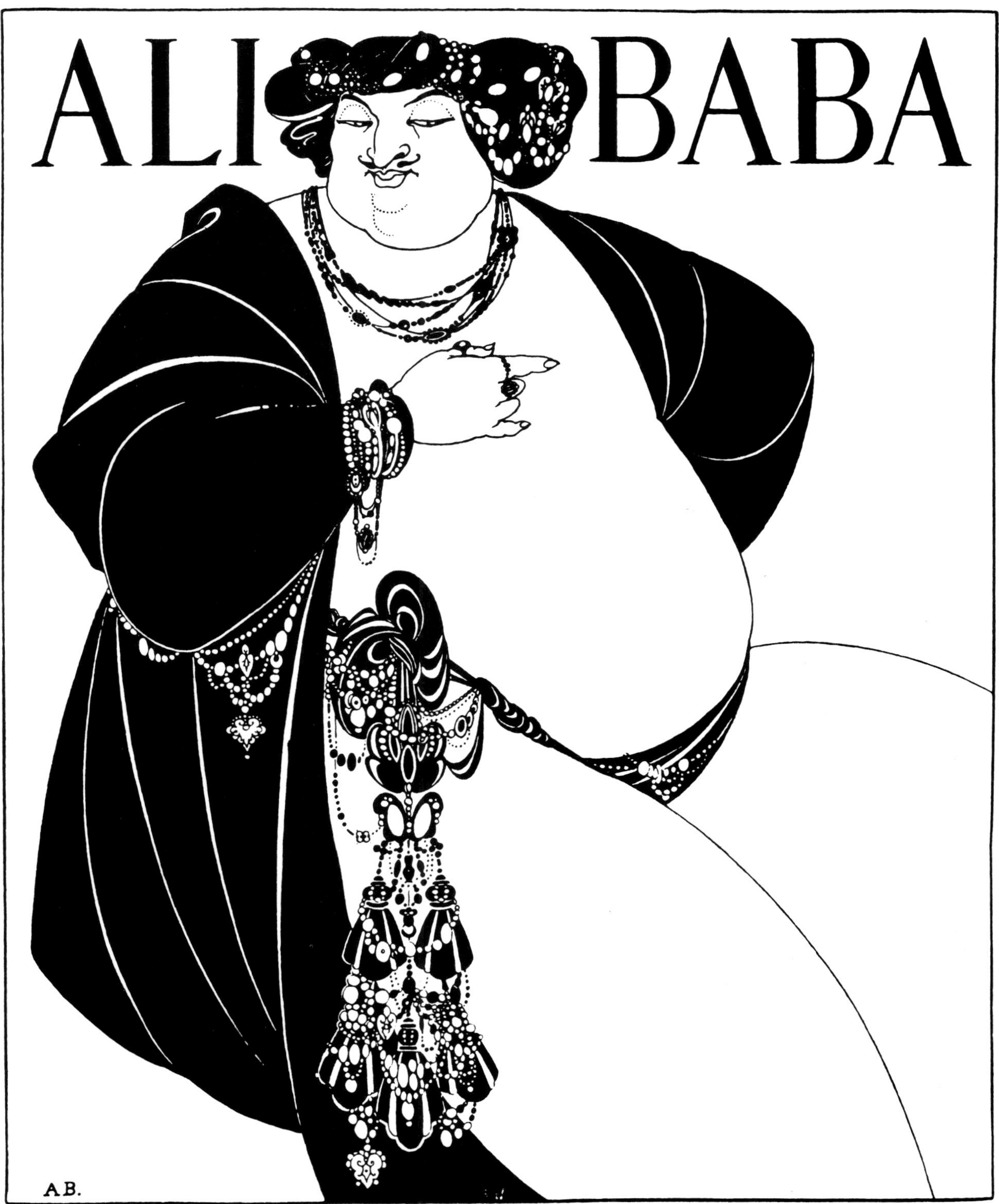

ALI BABA
A.B.

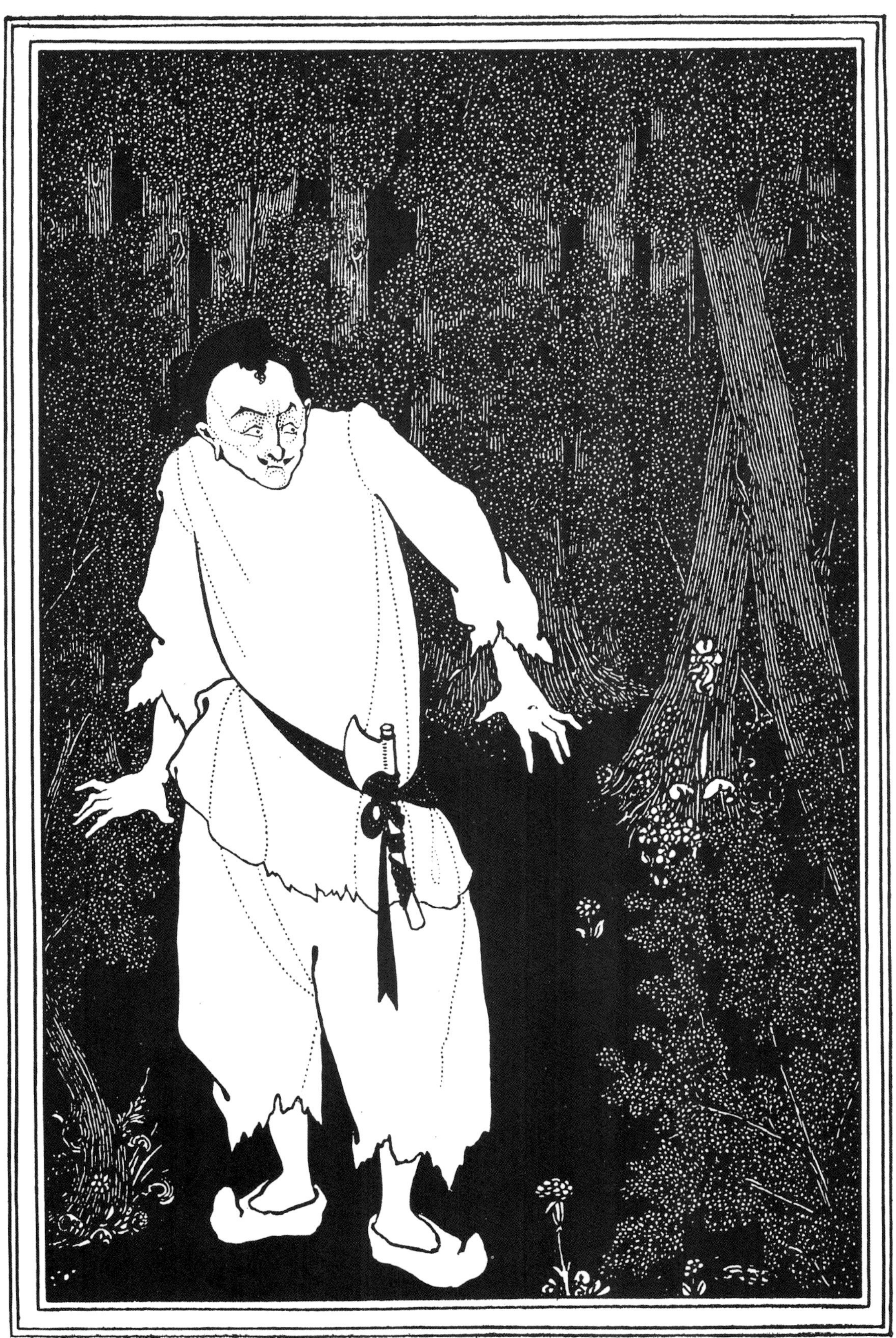

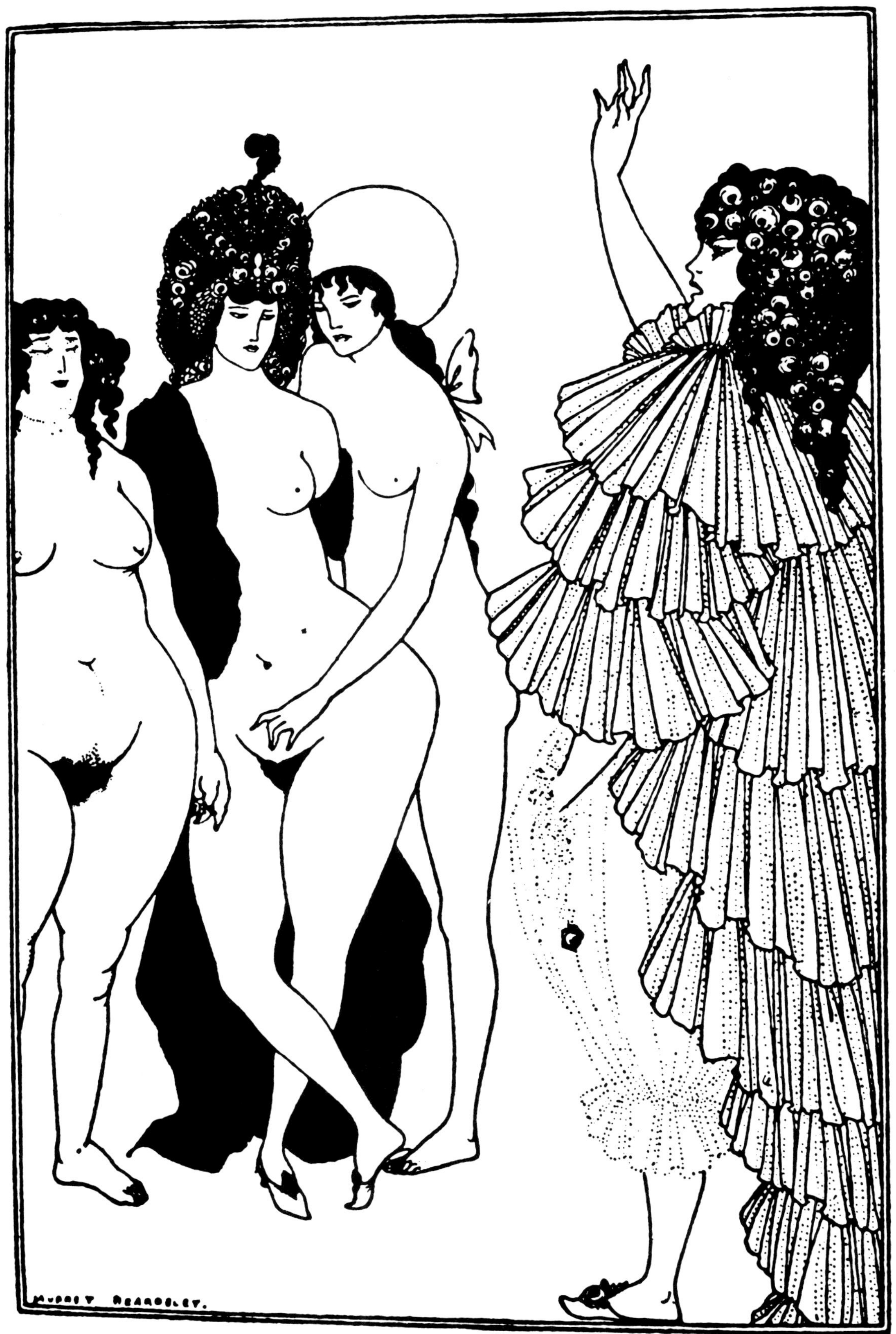

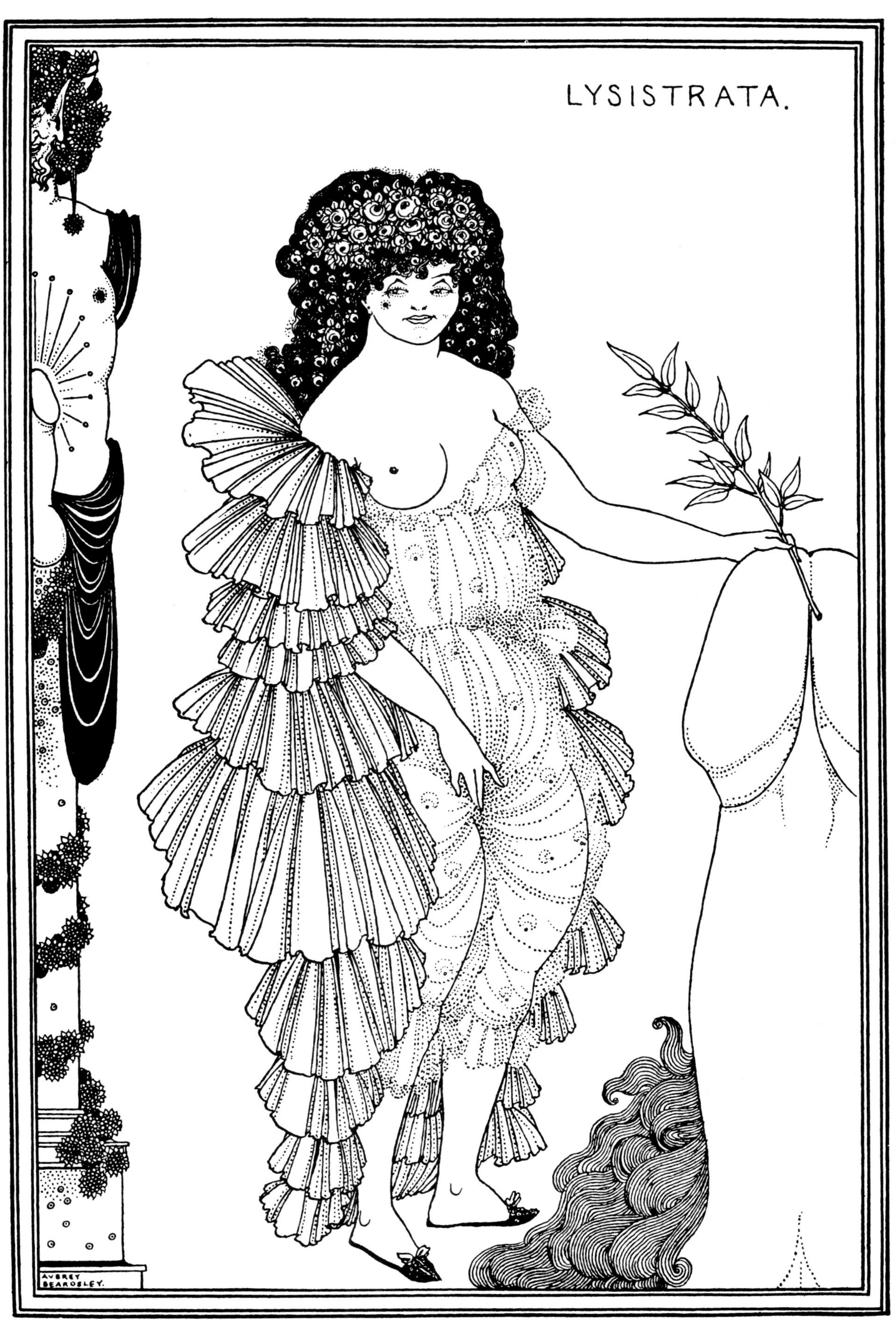

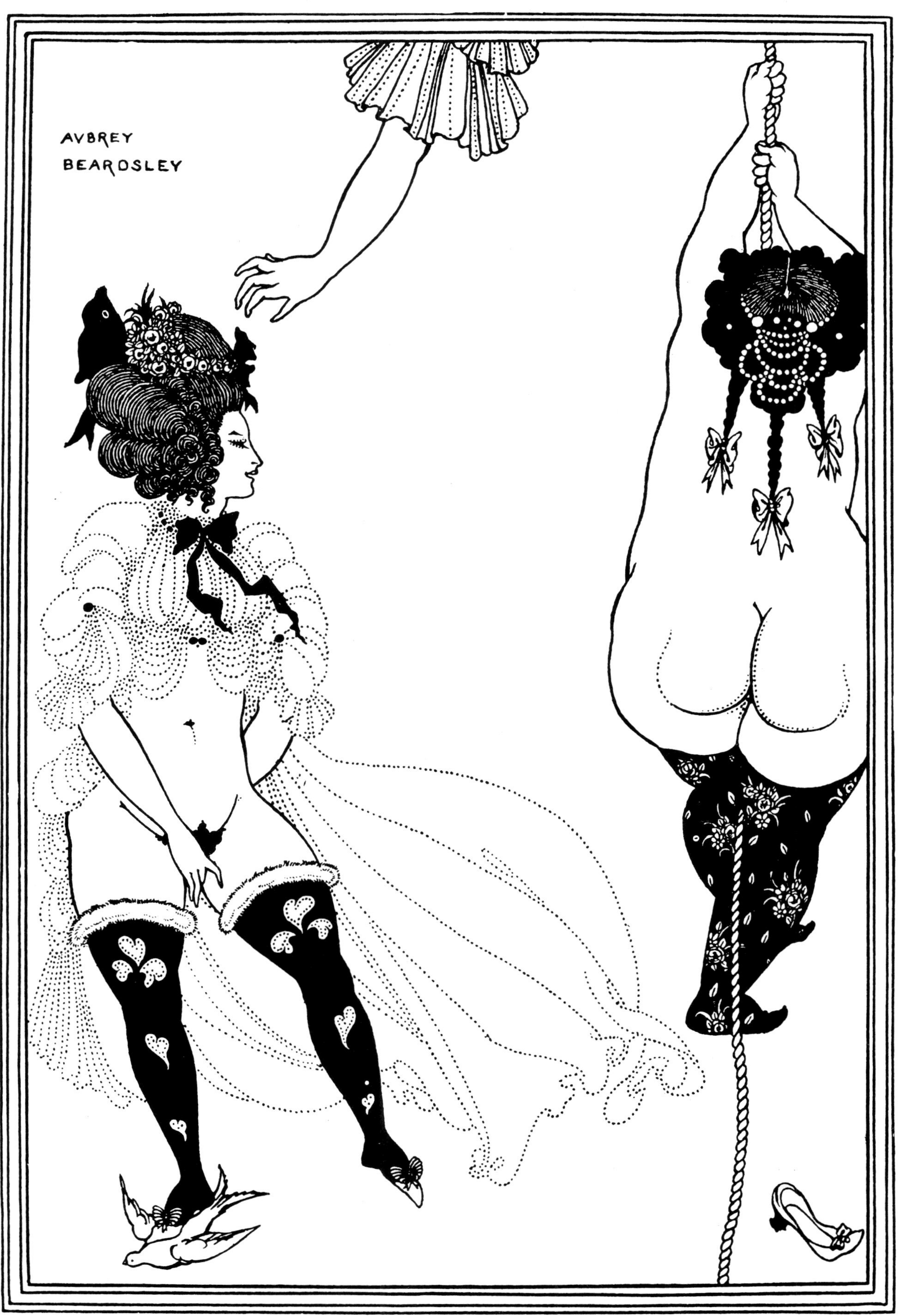
AVBREY
BEARDSLEY

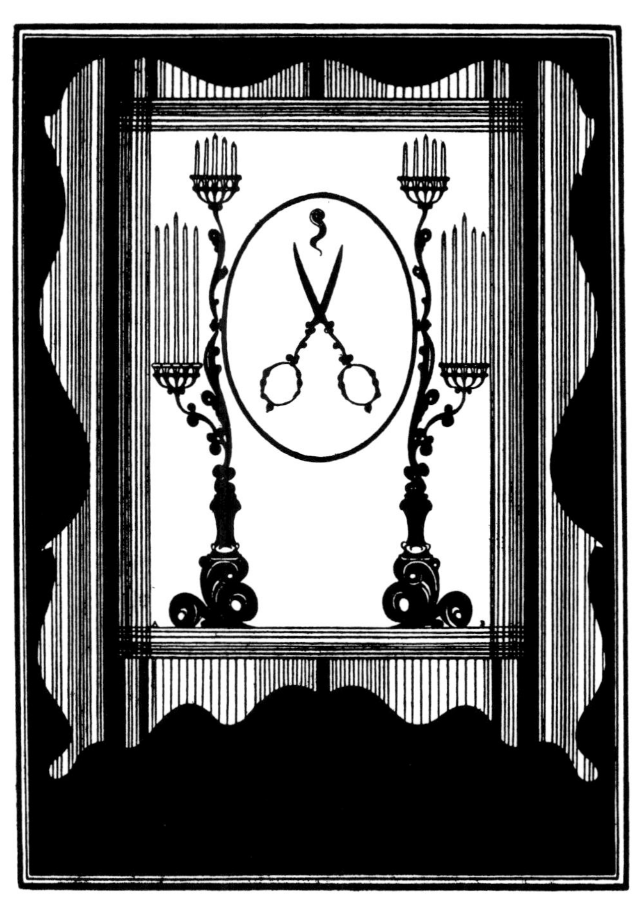

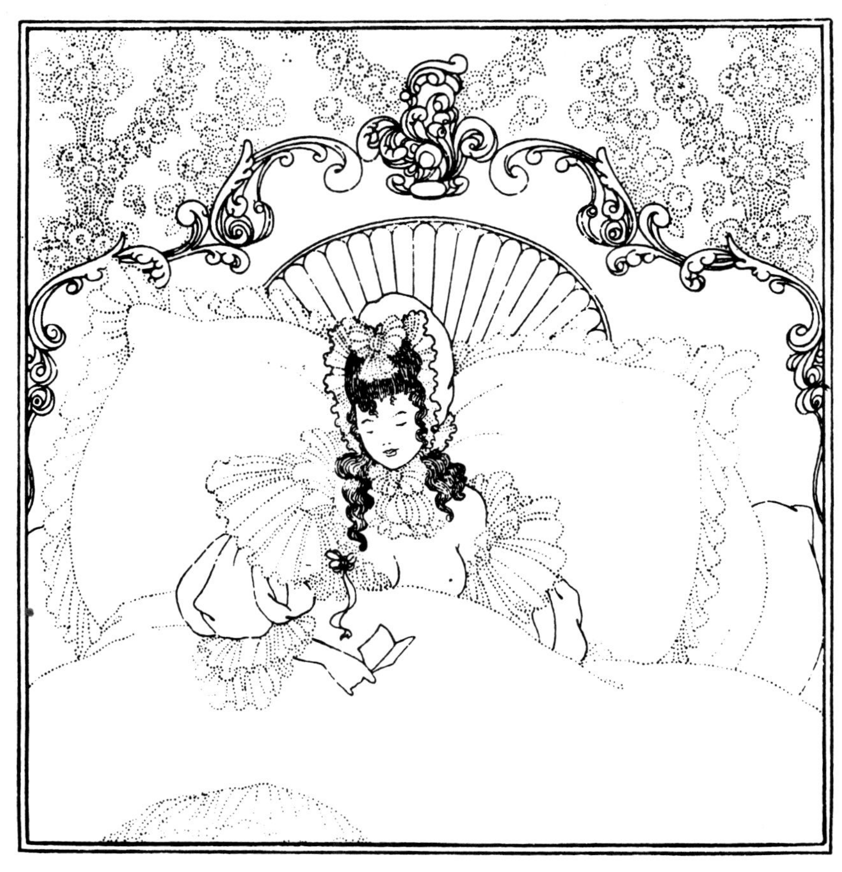

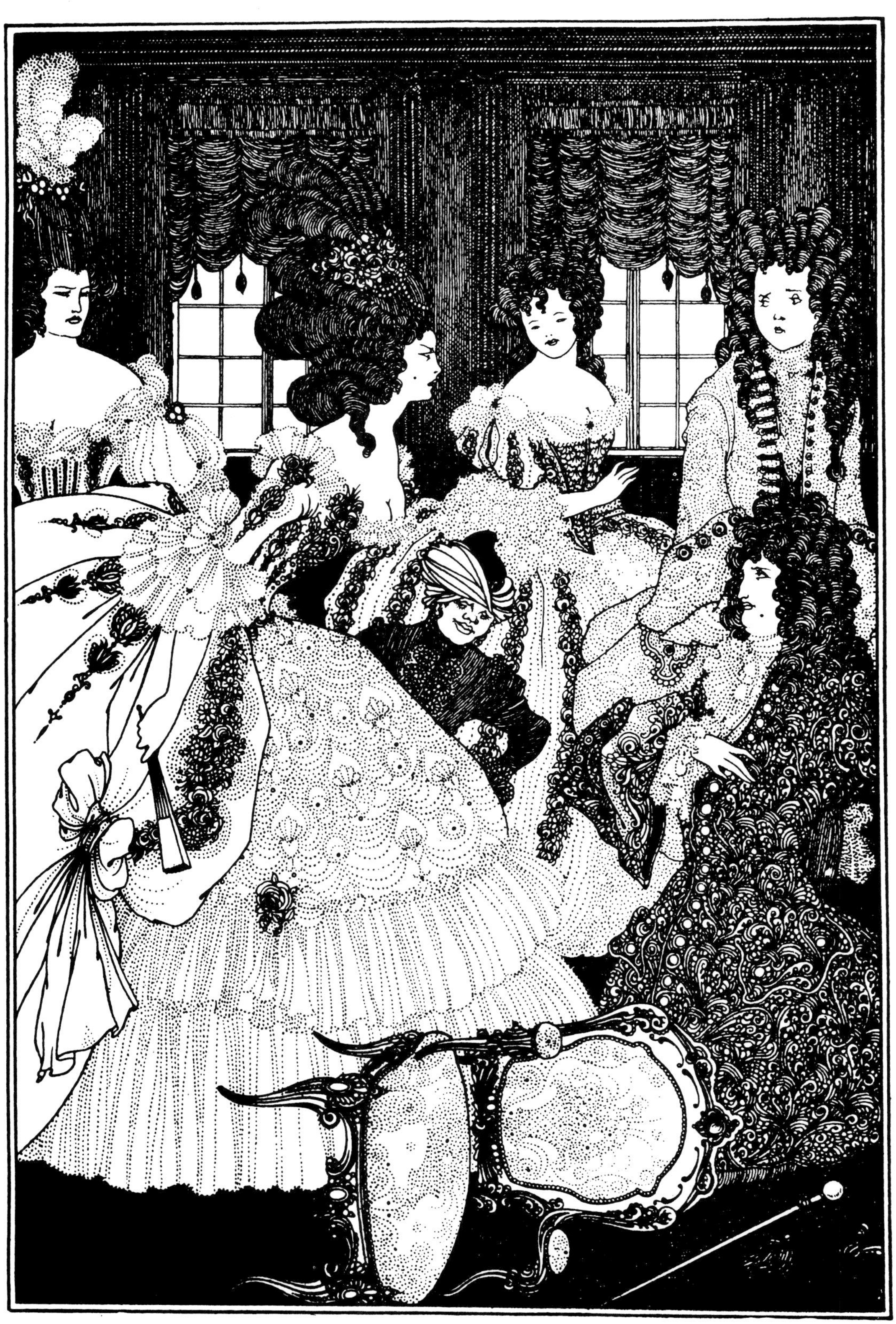

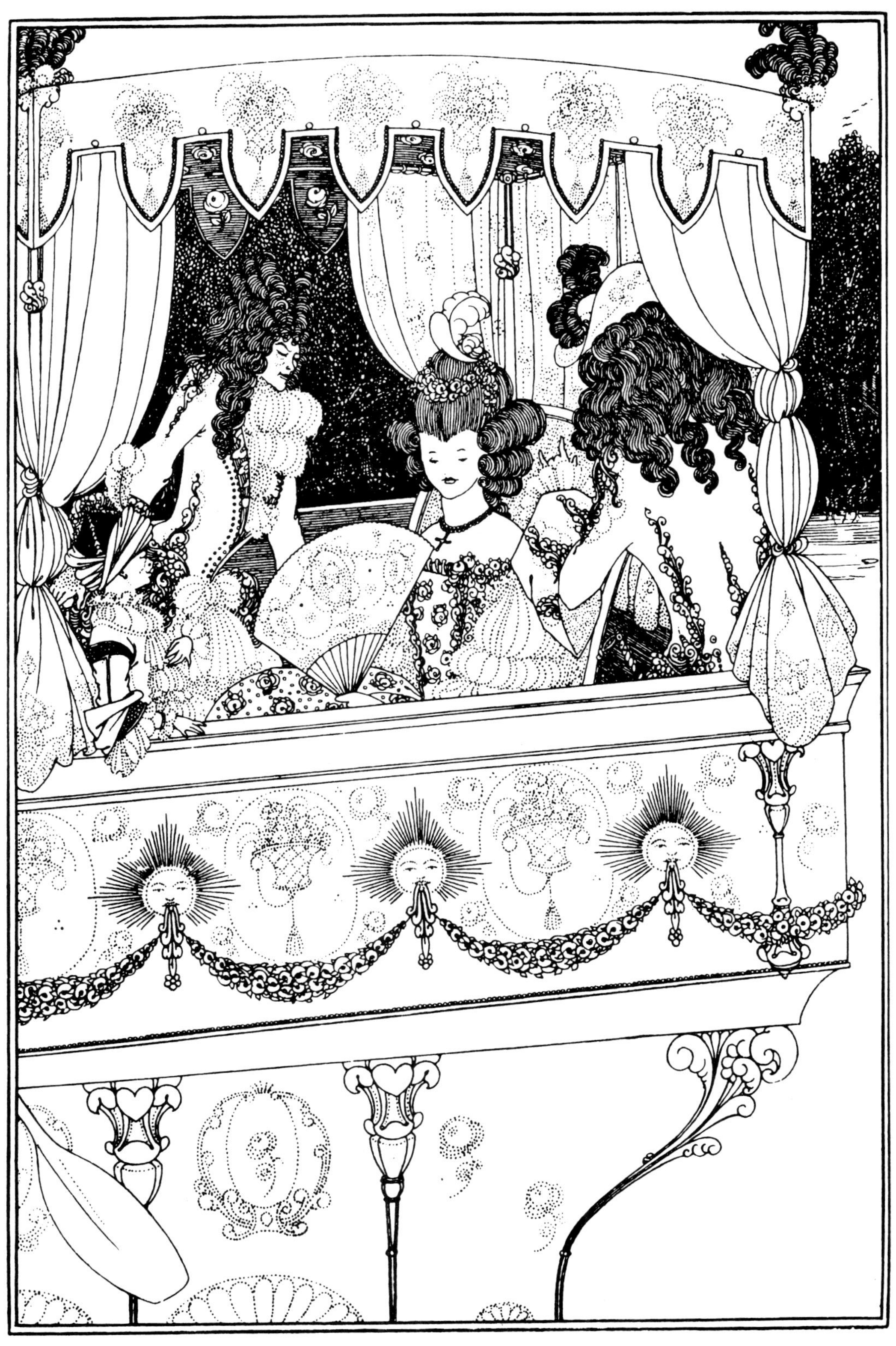

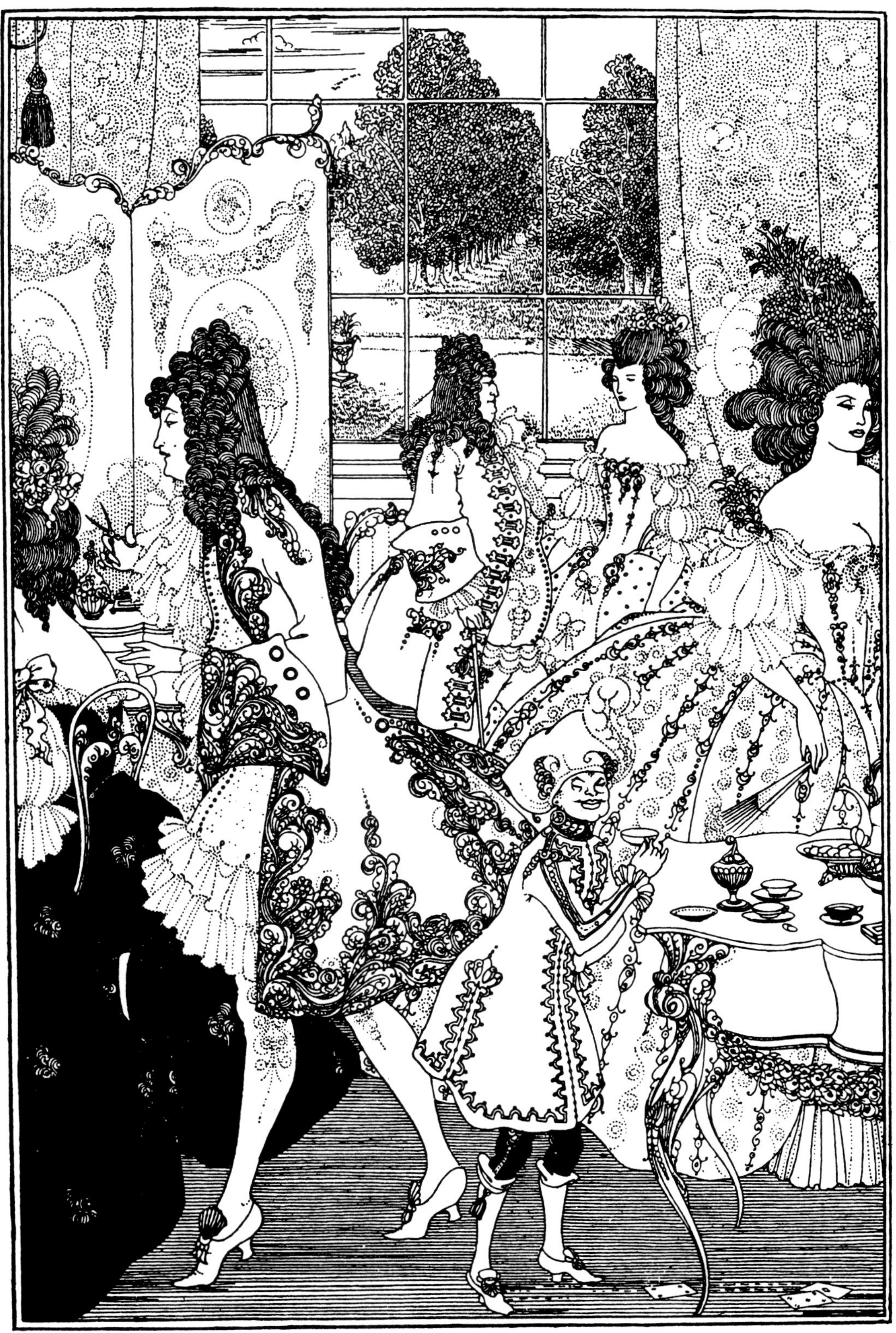

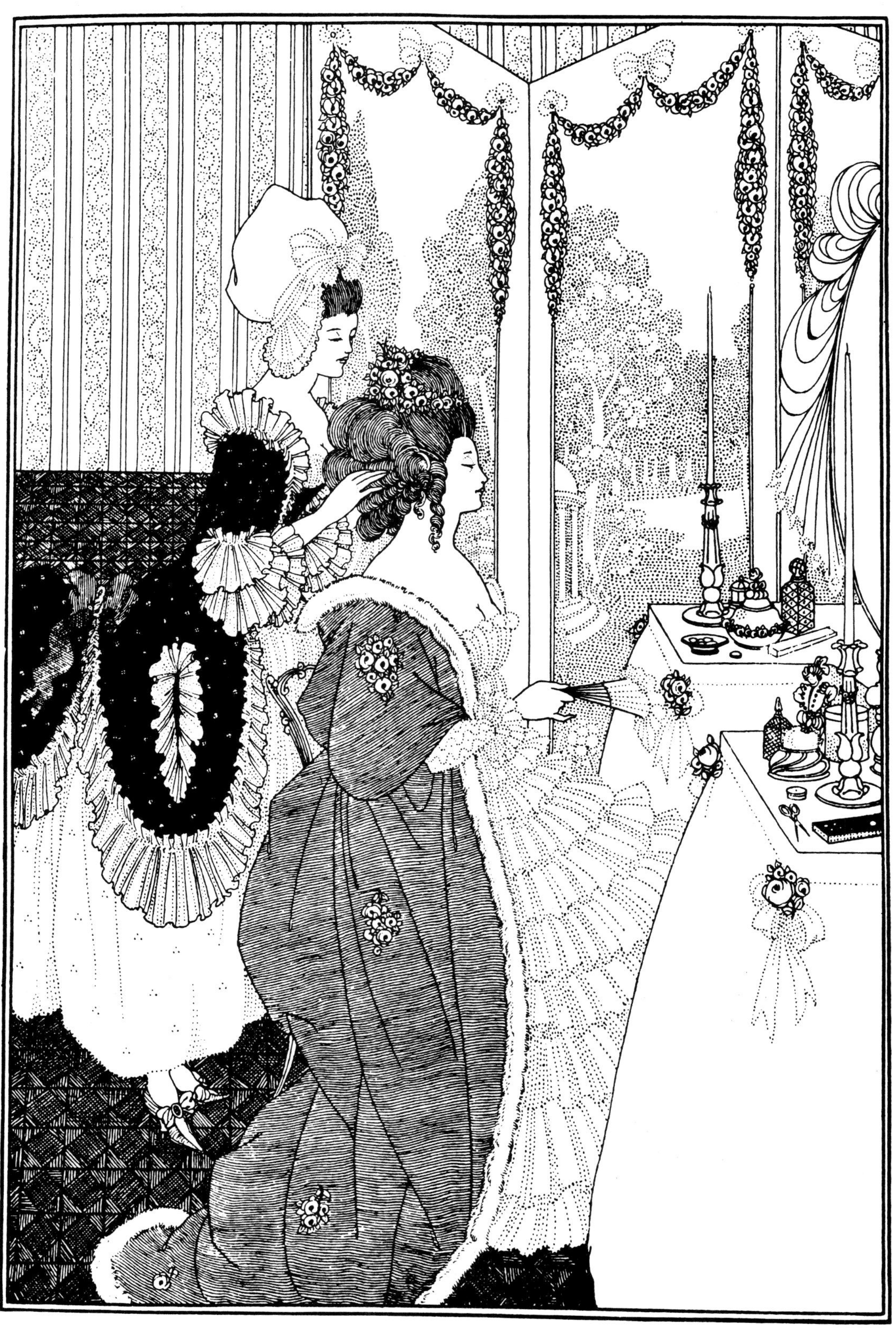

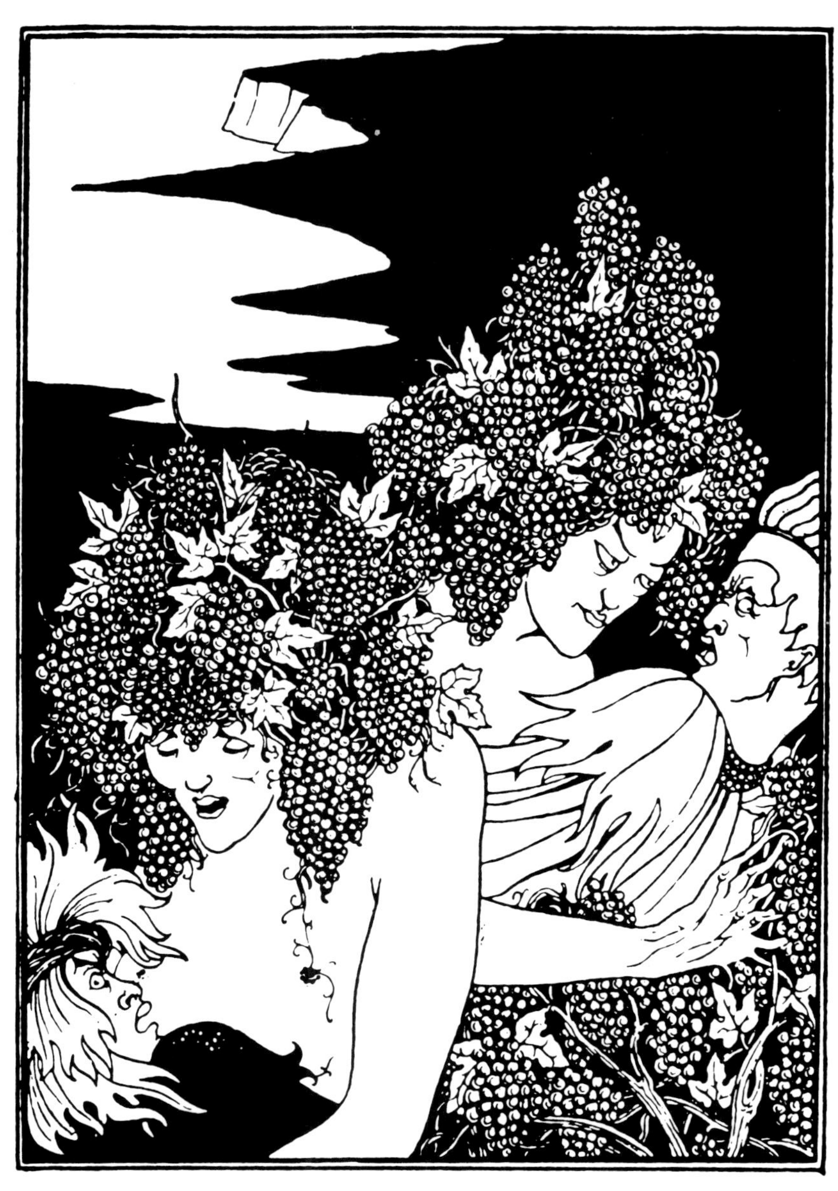

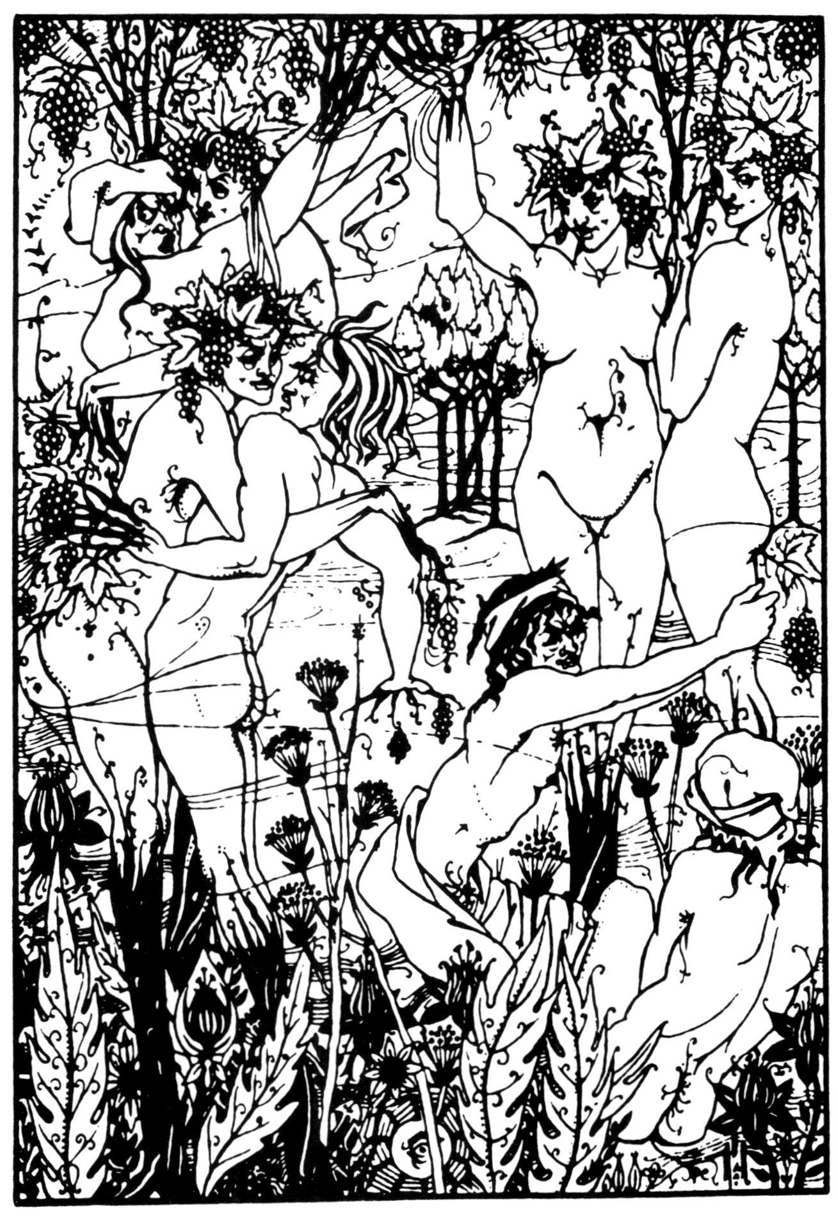

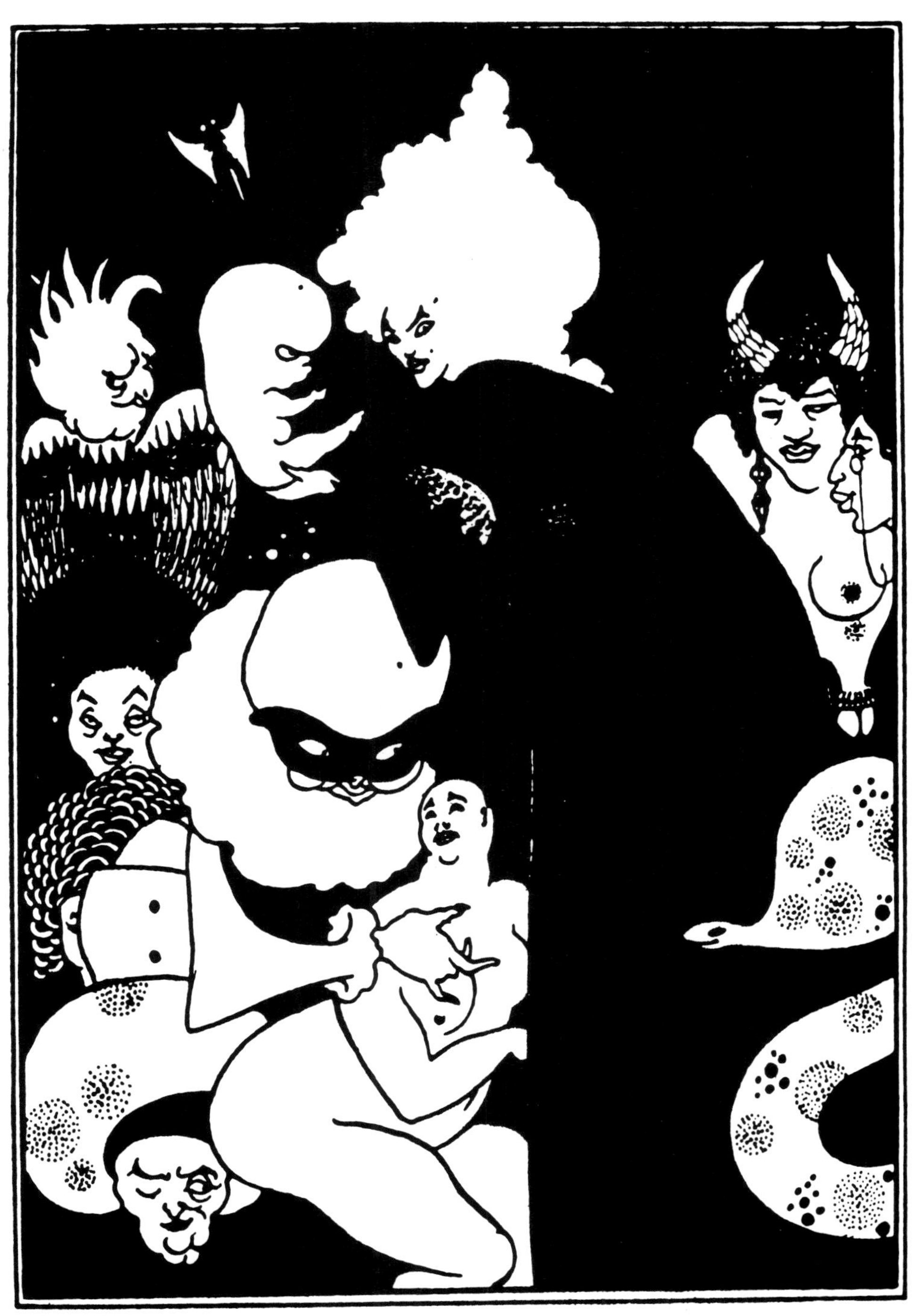

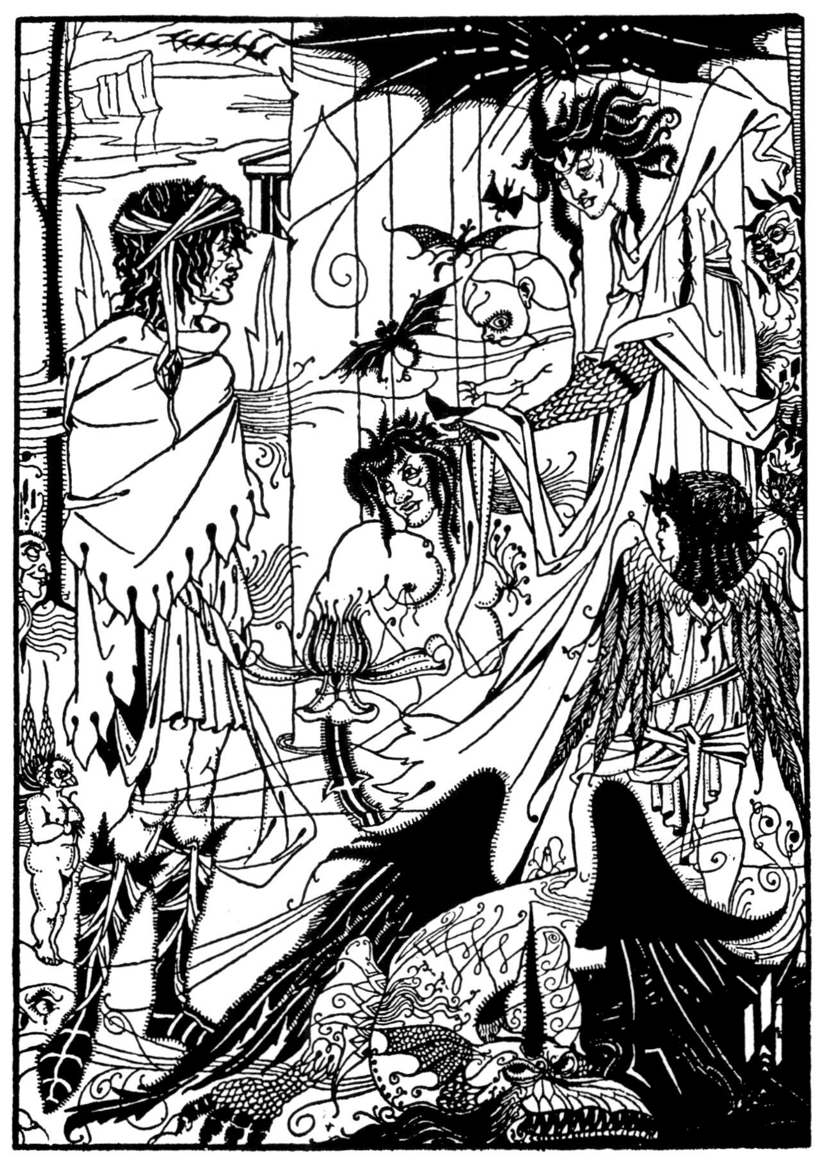

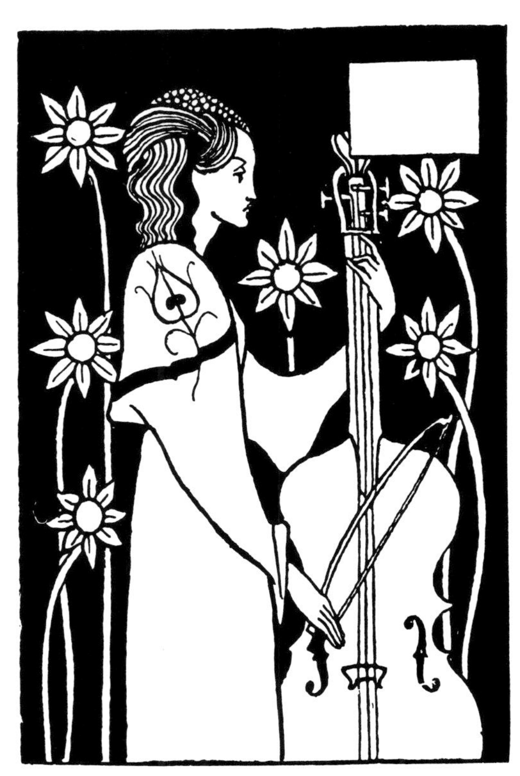

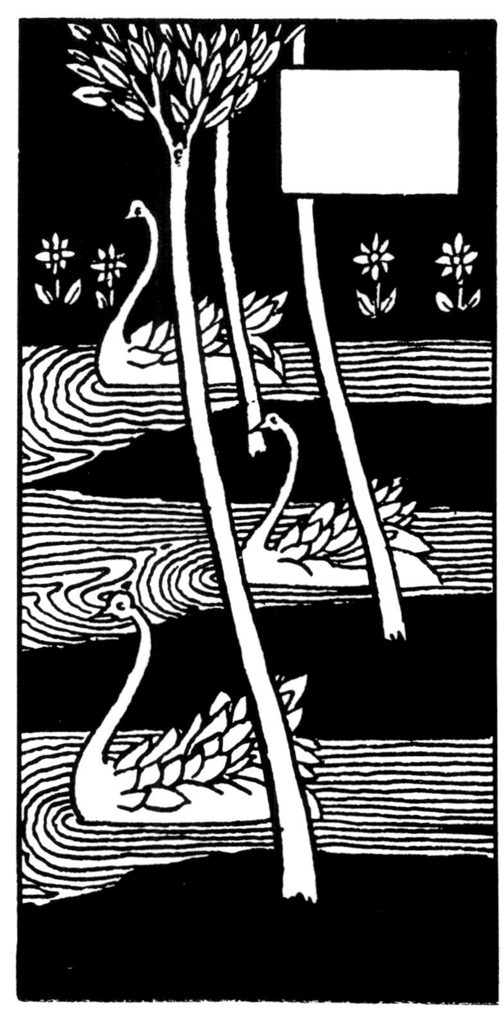

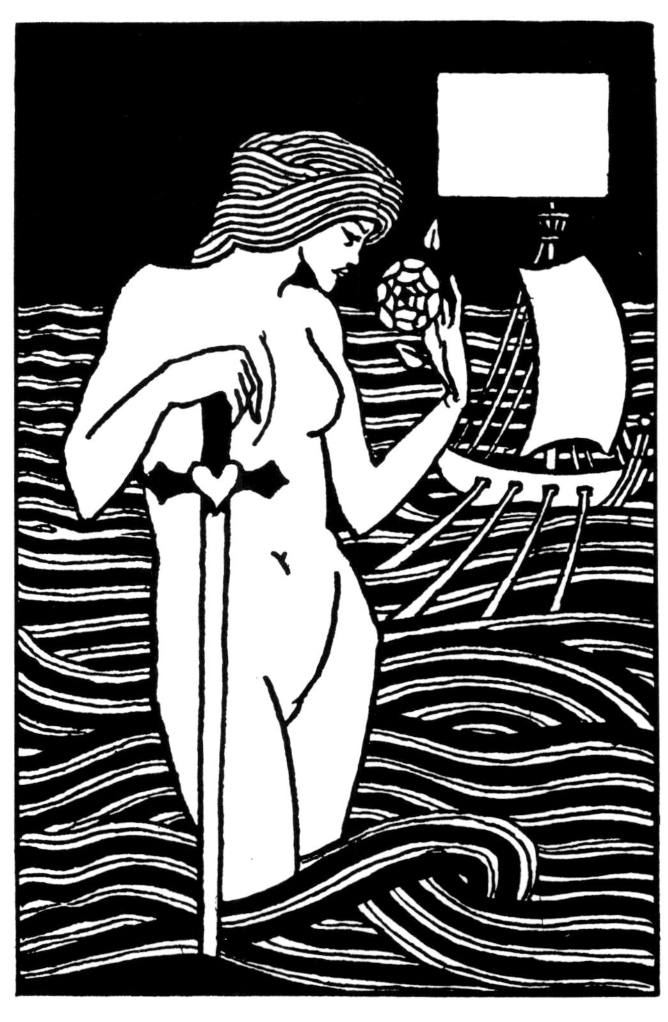

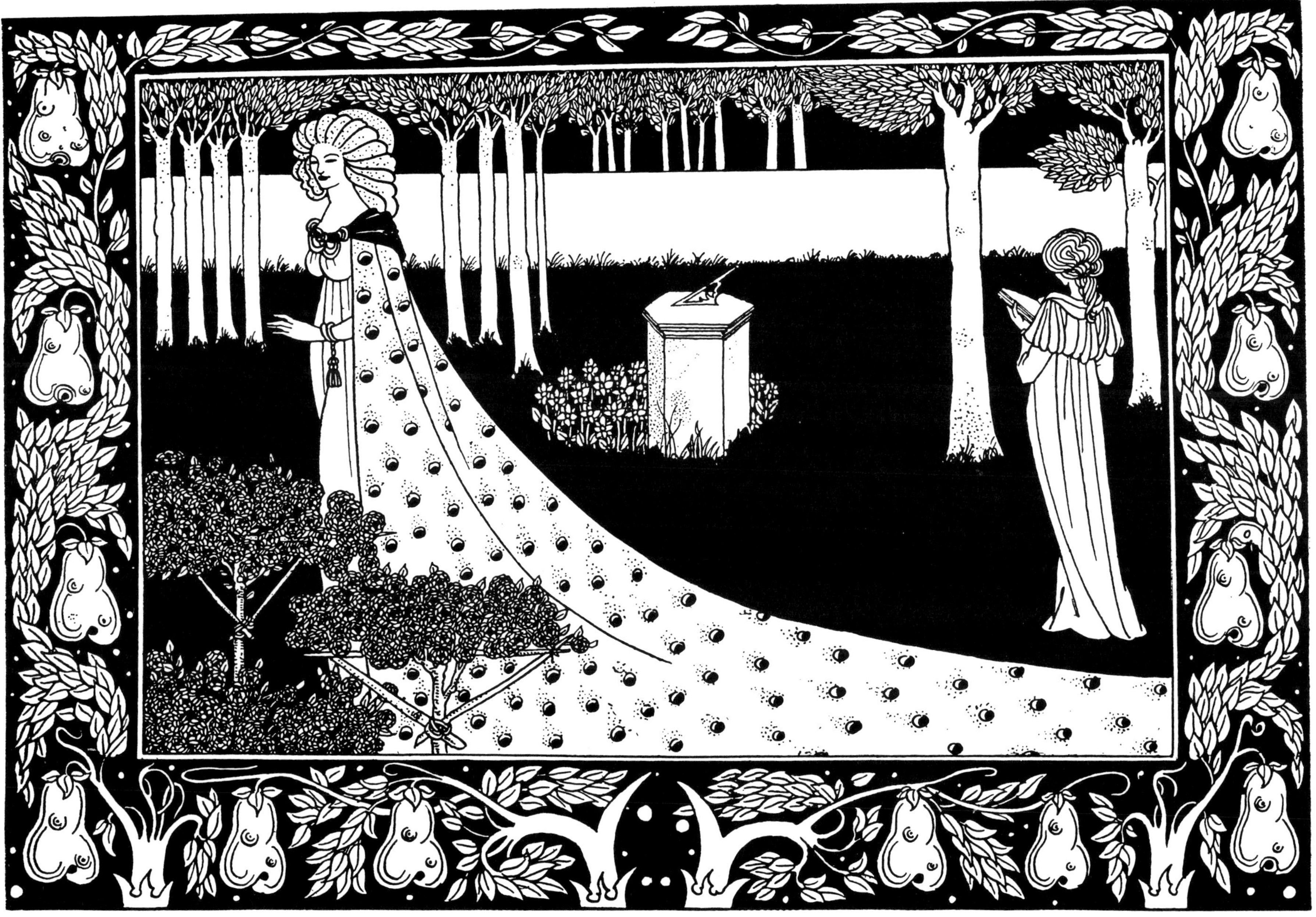

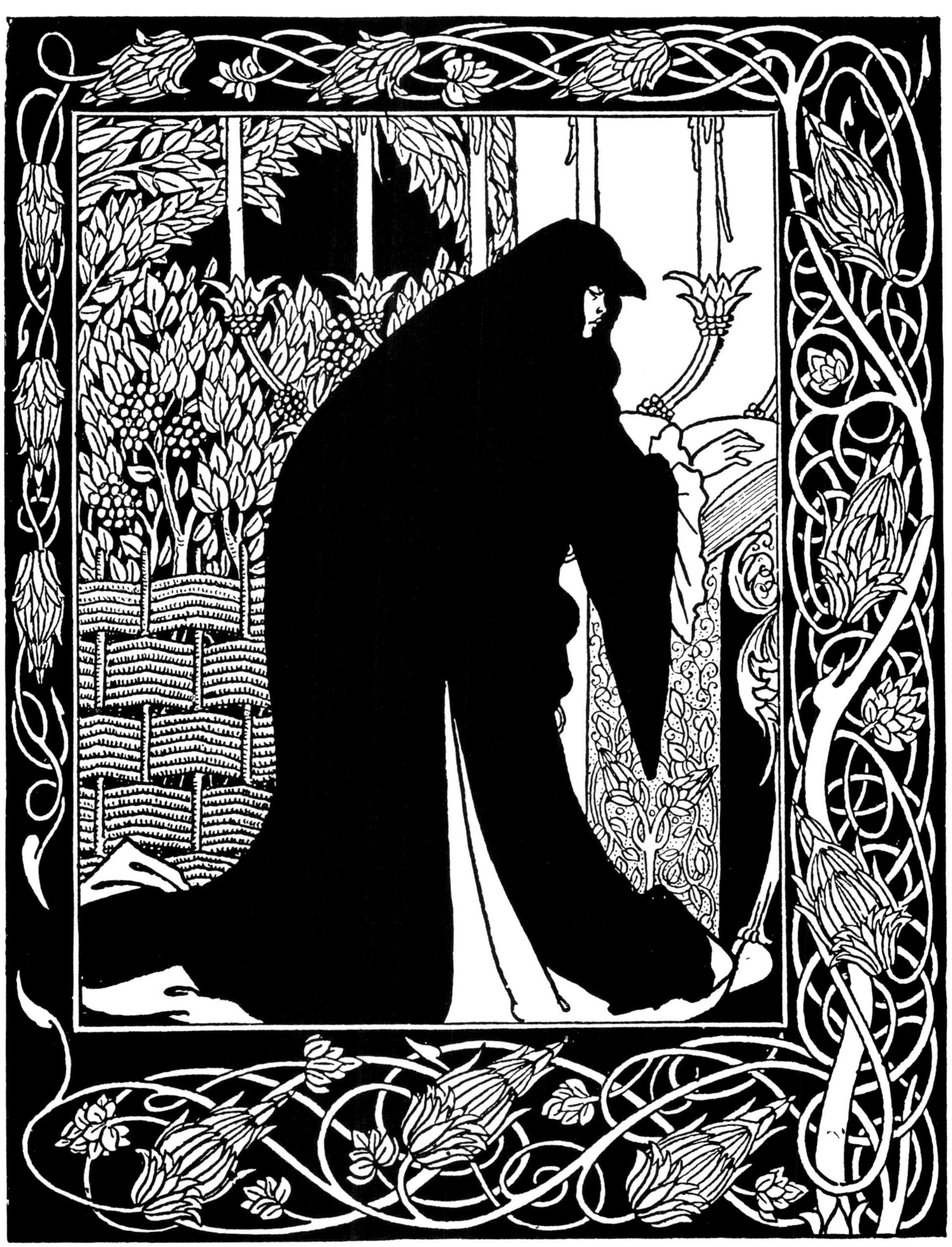

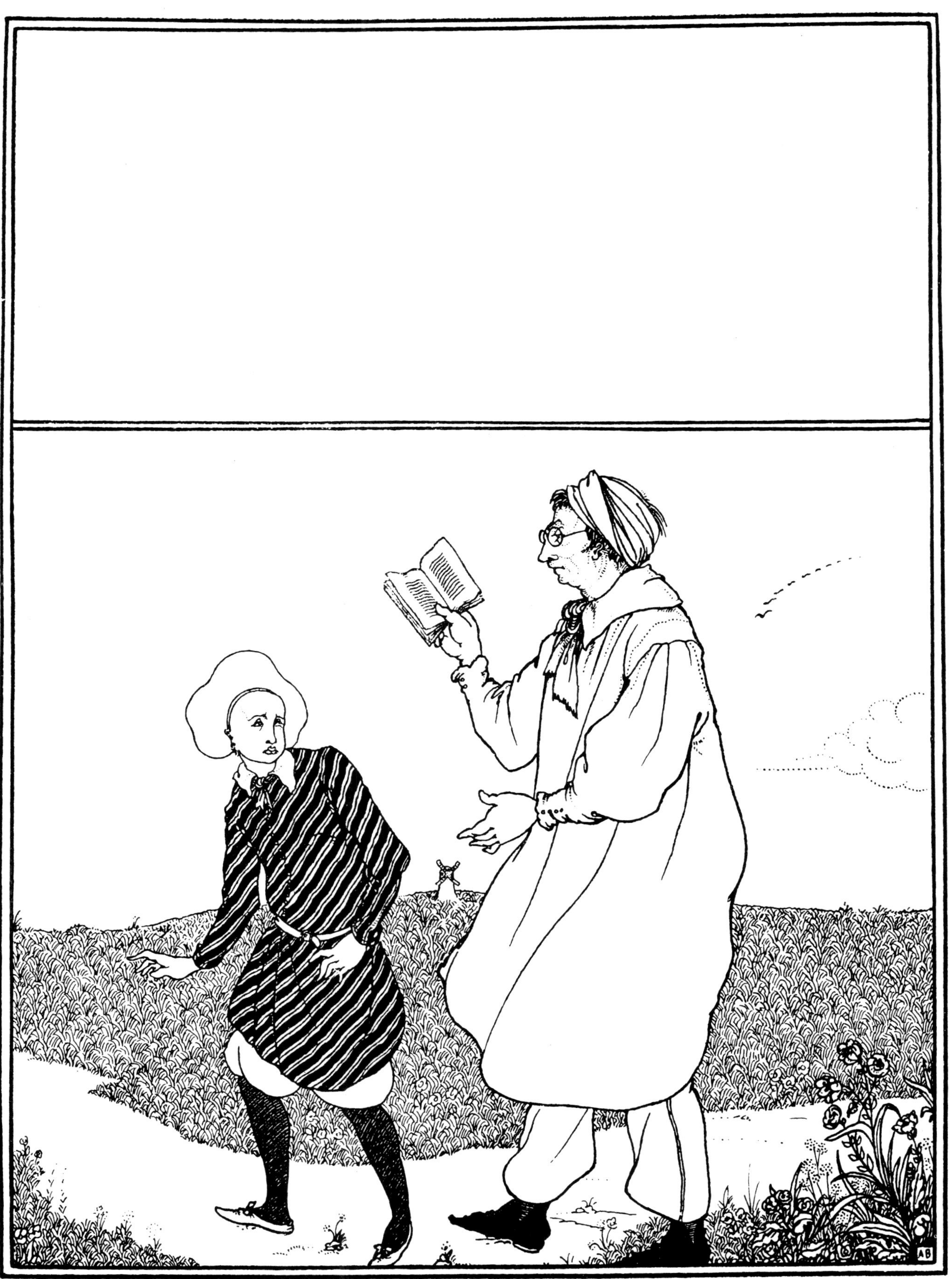

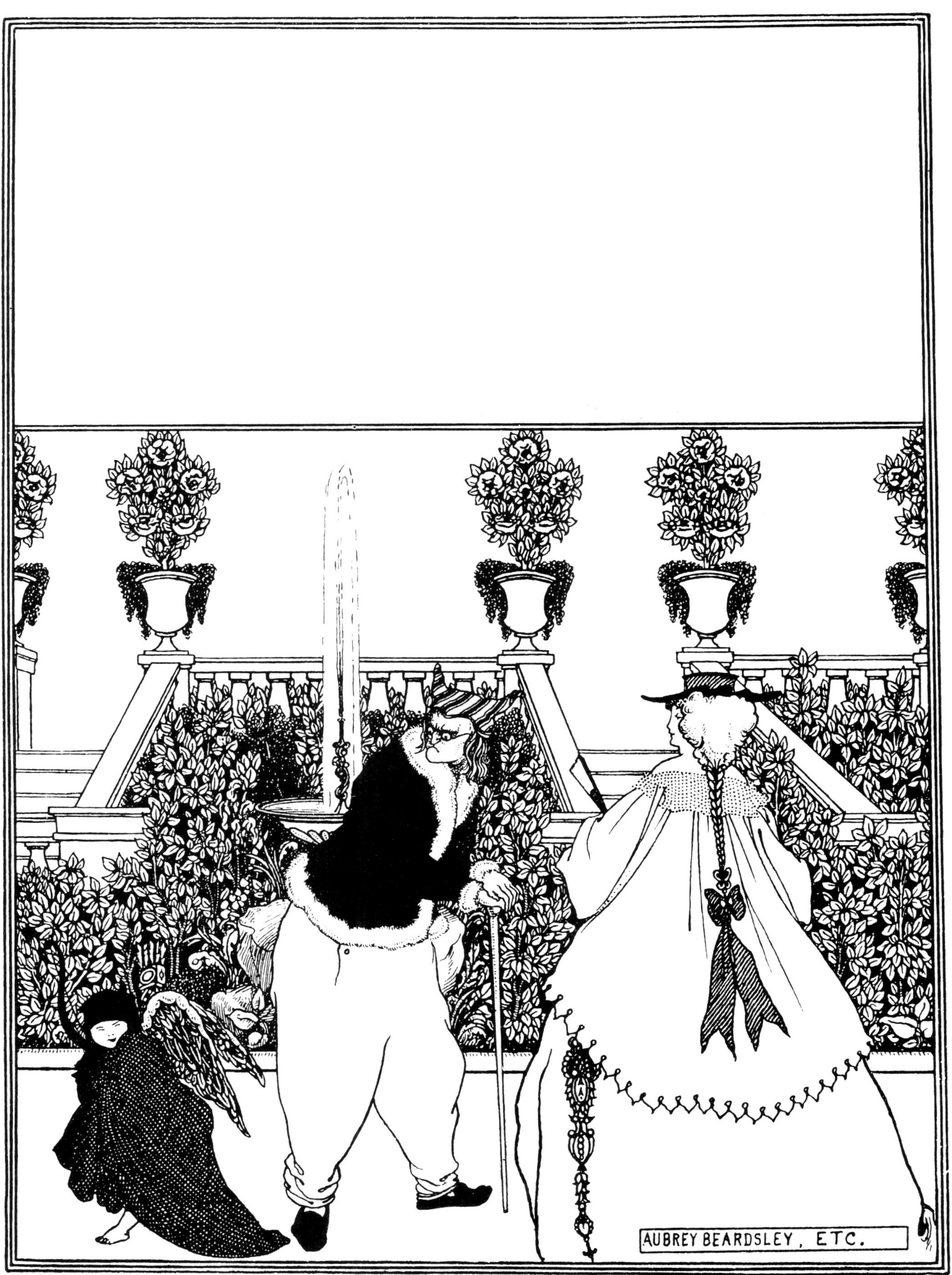
AUBREY BEARDSLEY, ETC.

THE
SAVOY

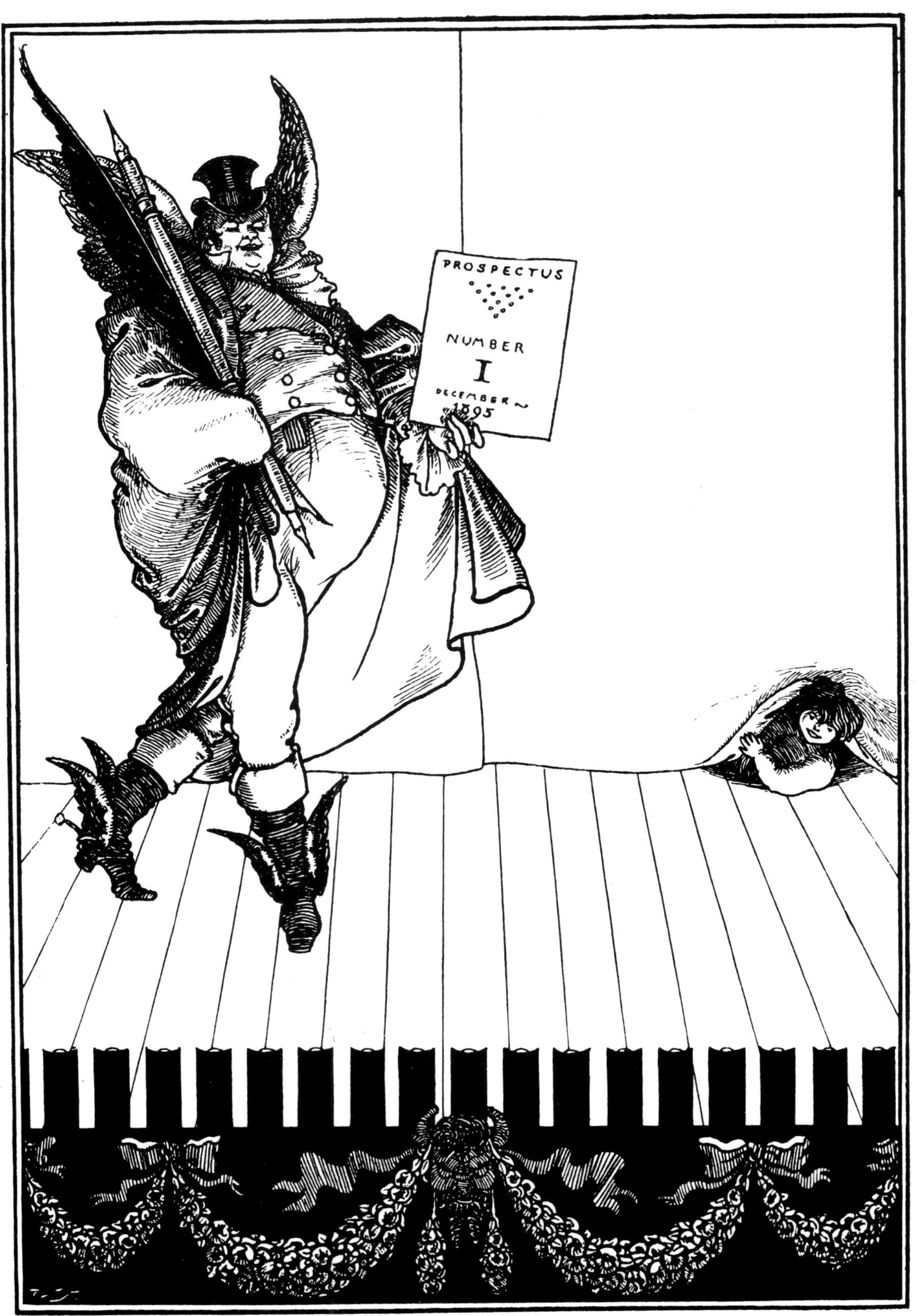

PROSPECTUS
NUMBER
I
DECEMBER ~
1895

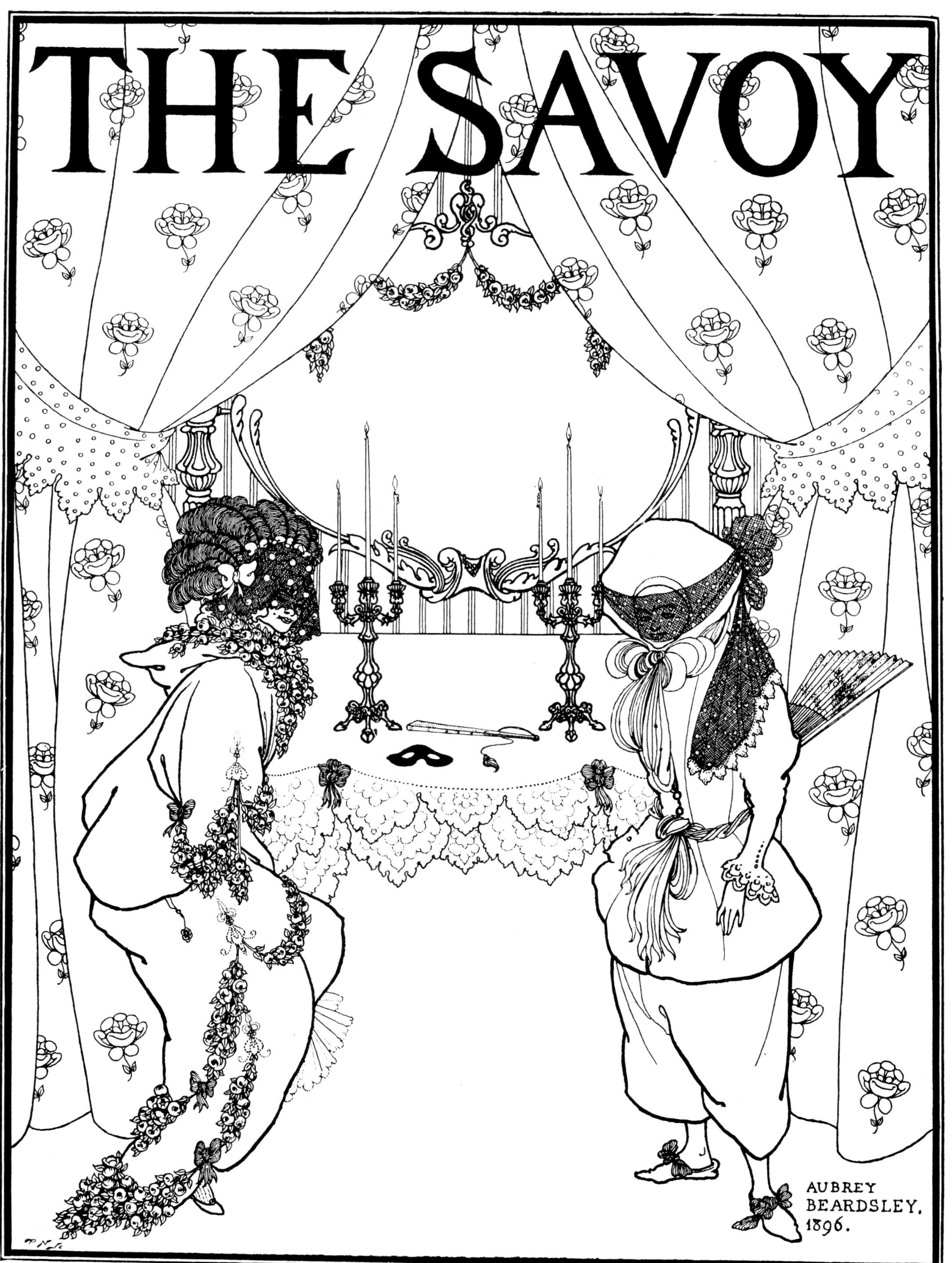

THE SAVOY
AUBREY
BEARDSLEY.
1896.

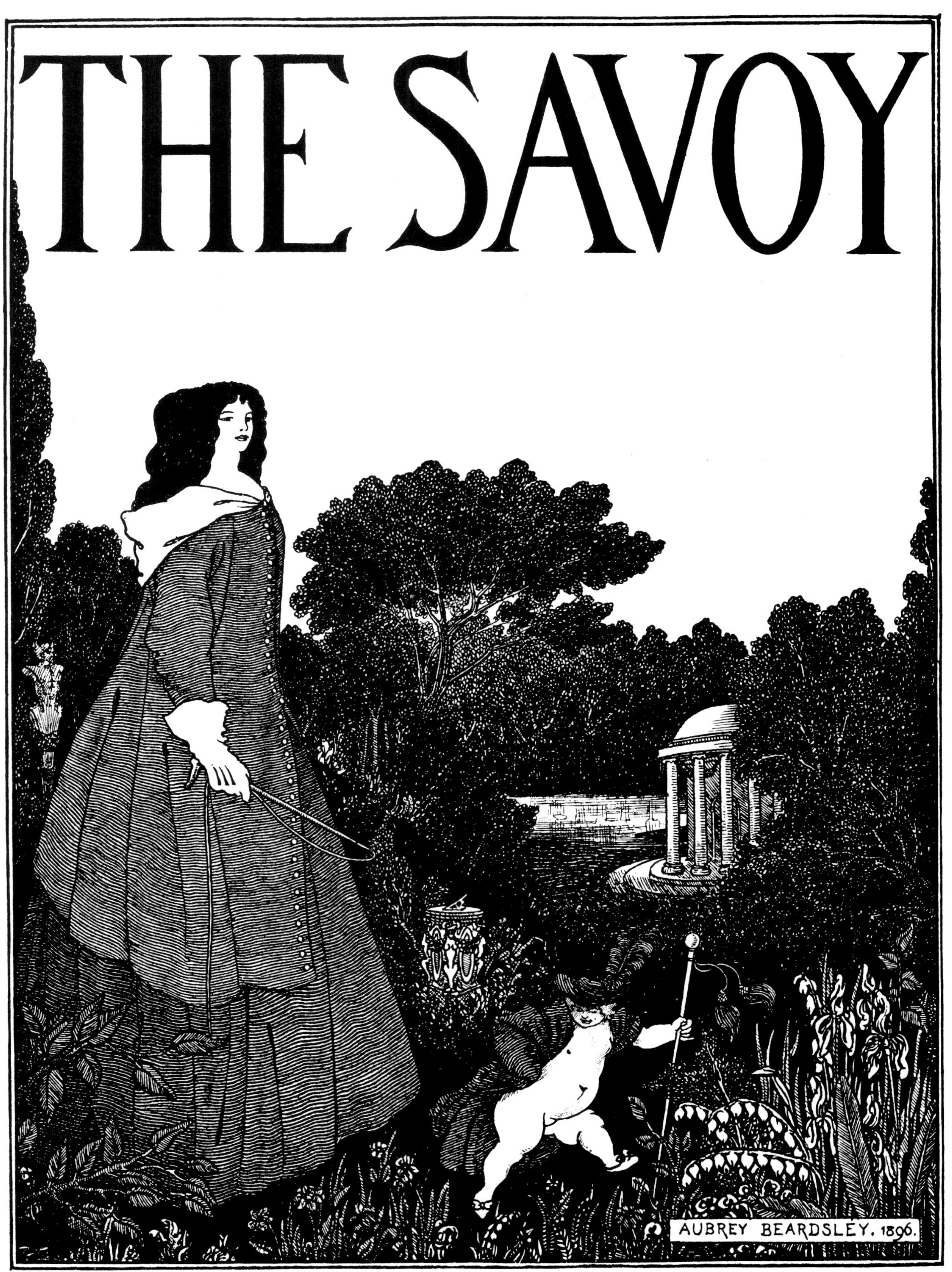

THE SAVOY

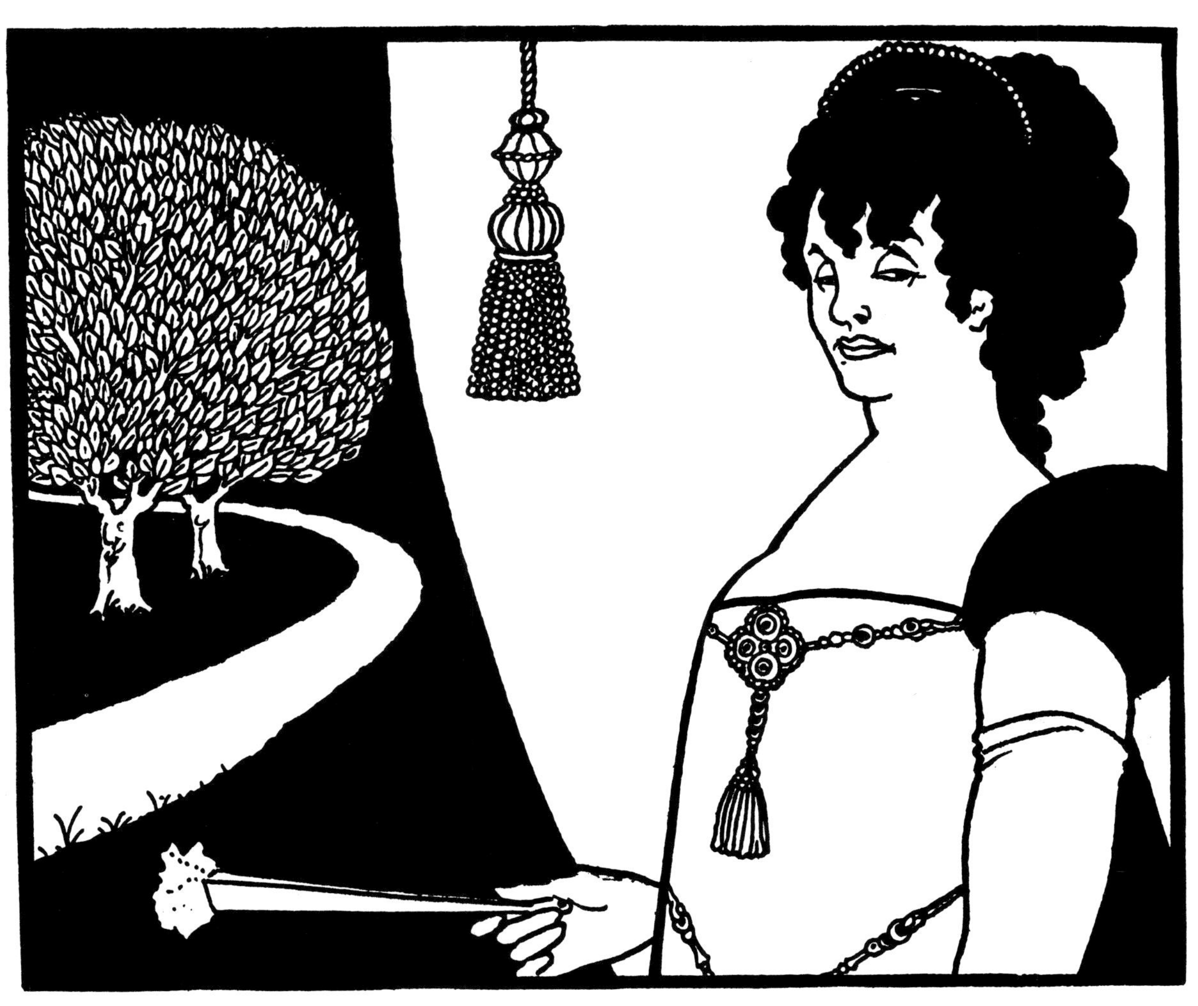

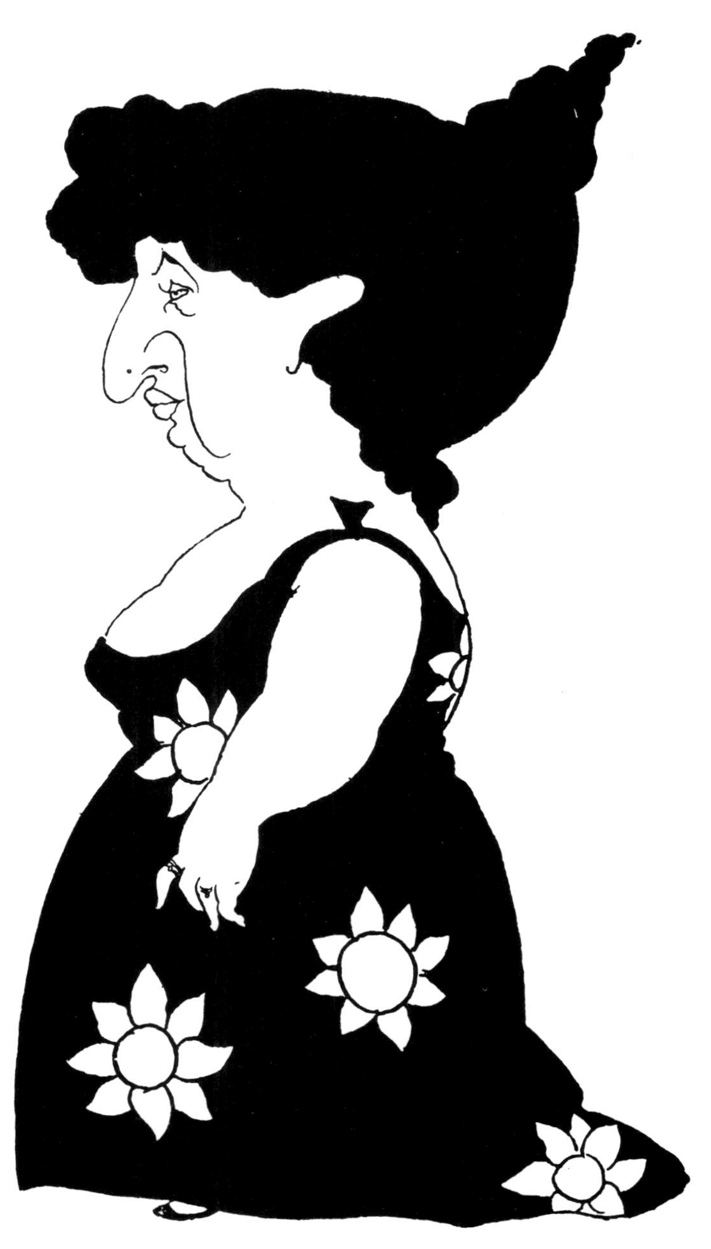

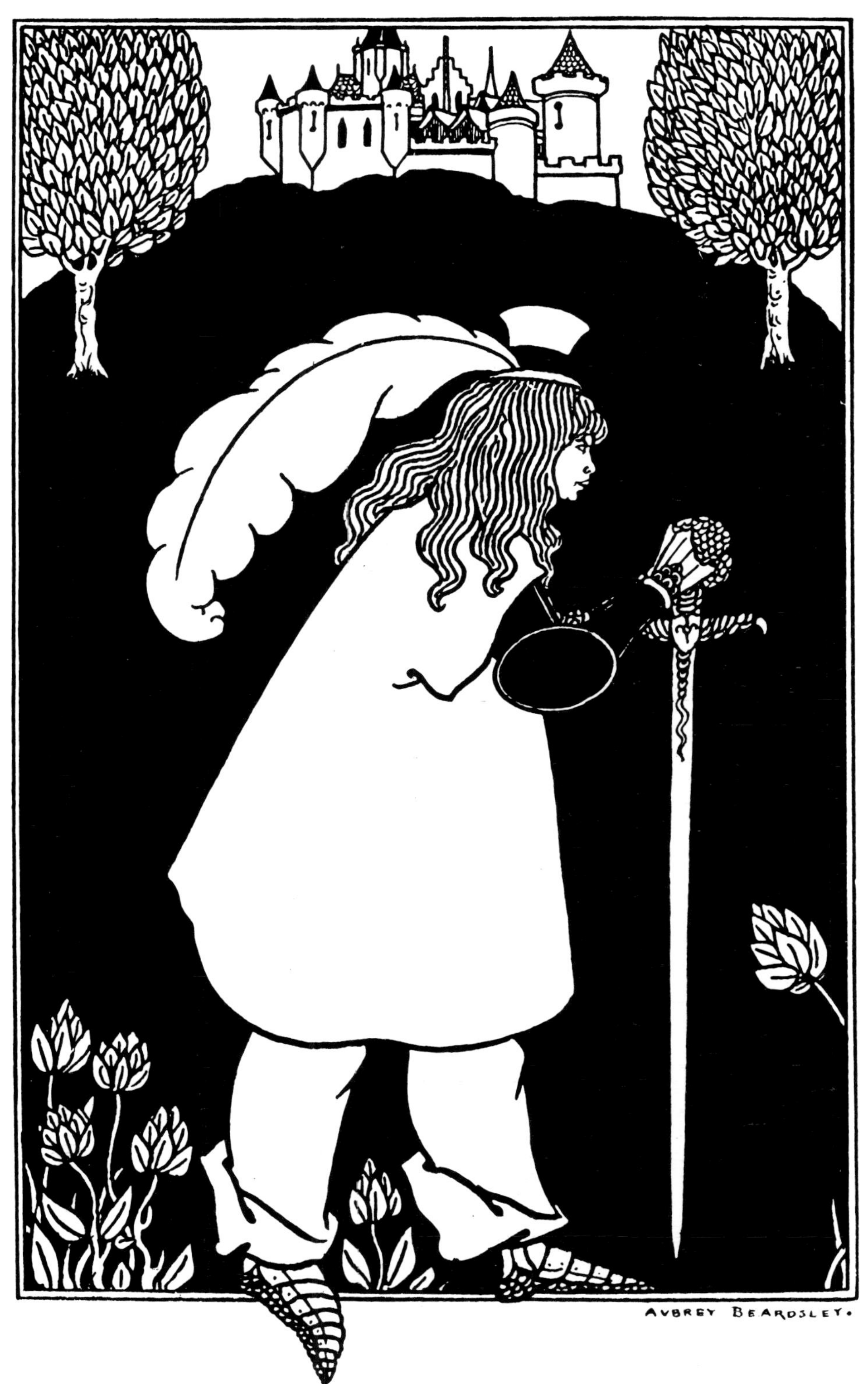

AUBREY BEARDSLEY.

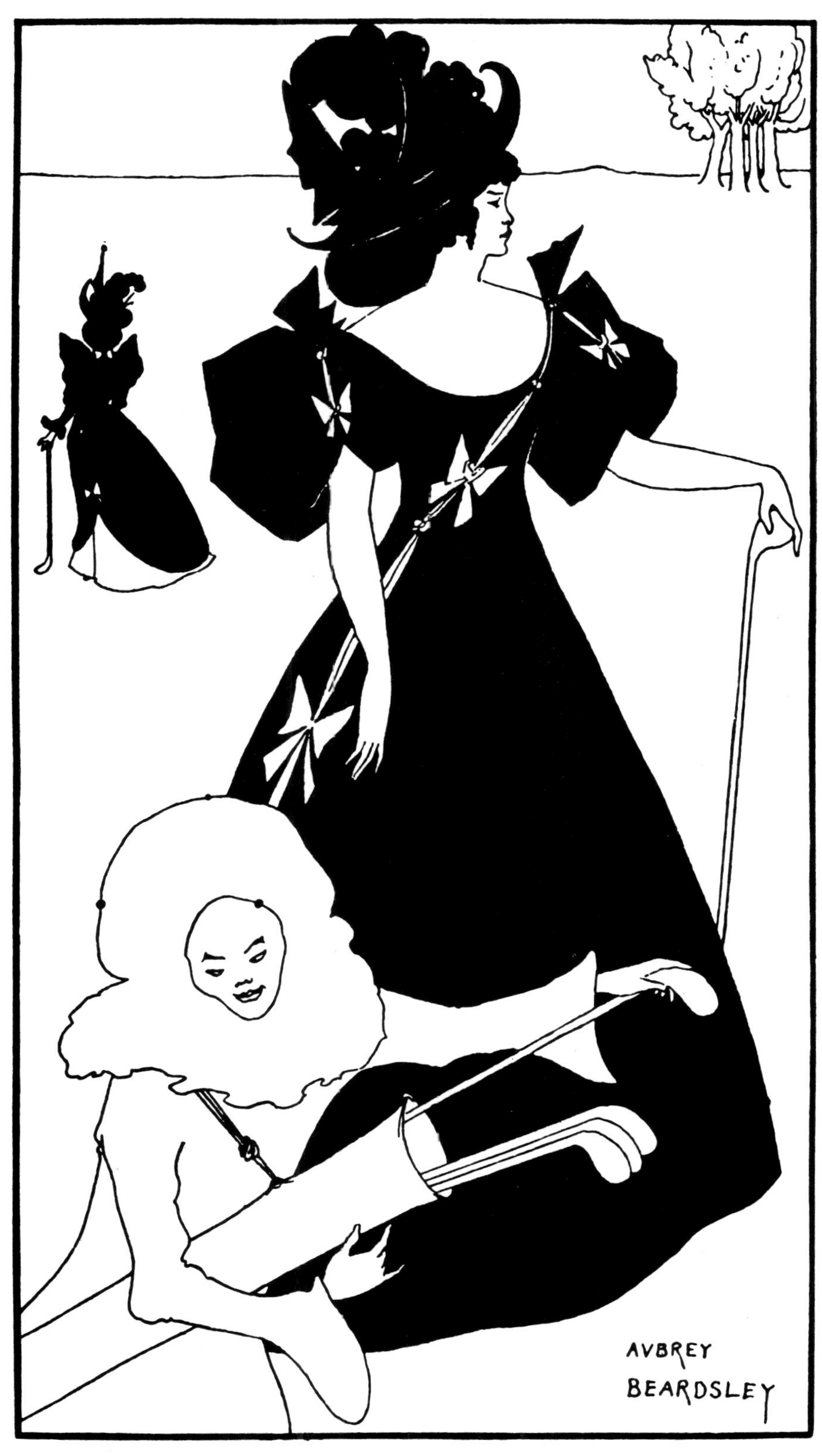

AVBREY
BEARDSLEY

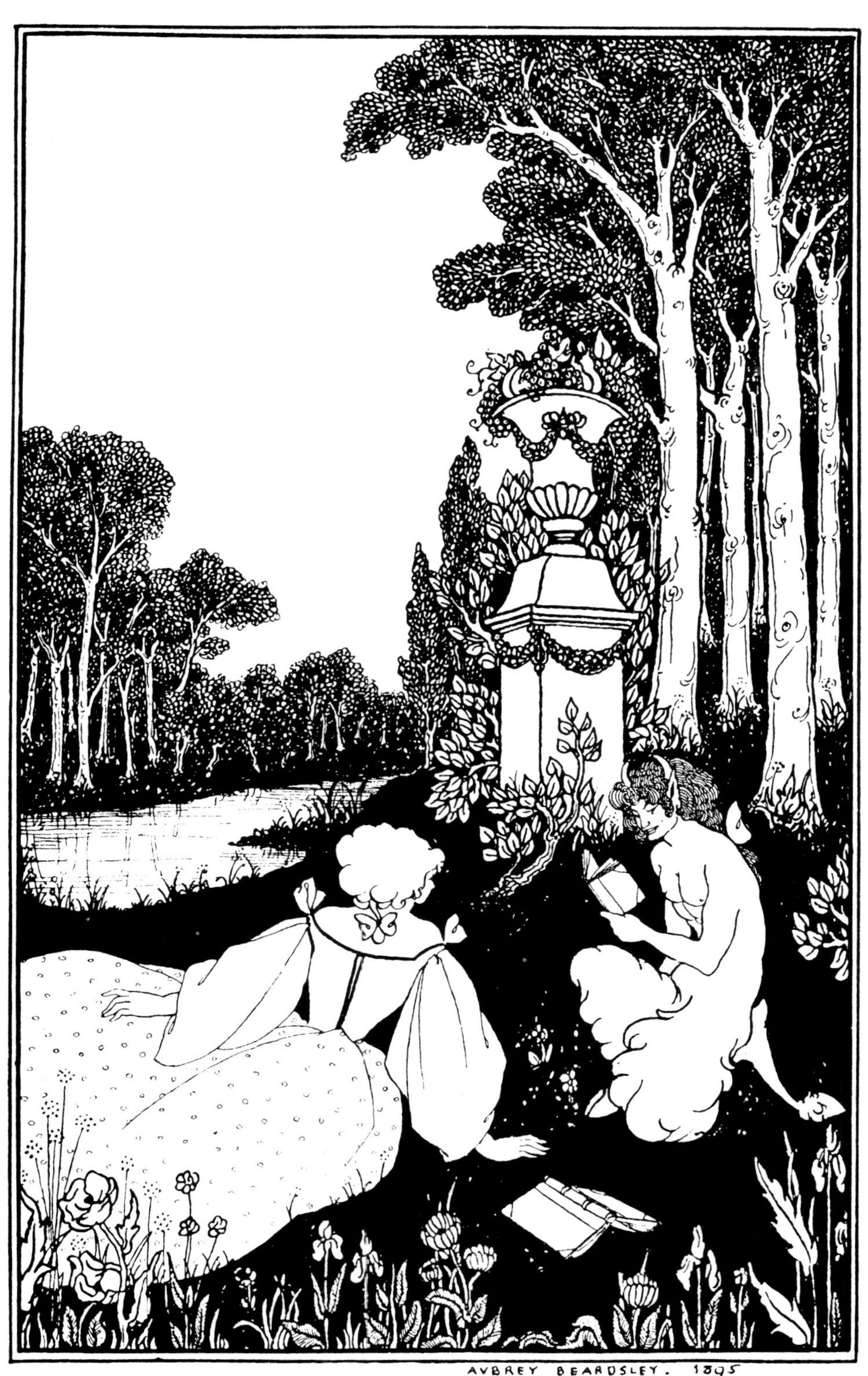

AVBREY BEARDSLEY. 1895

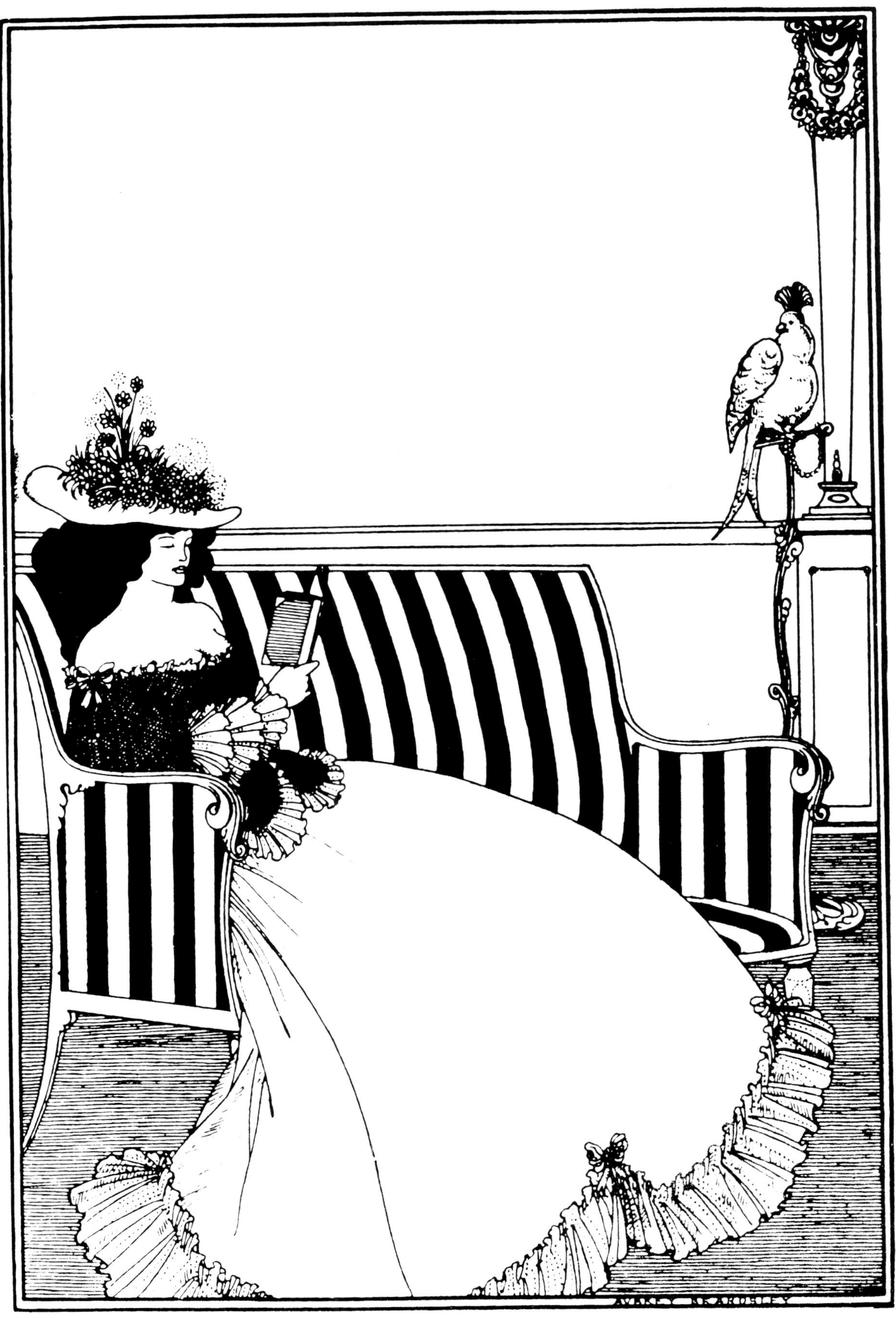

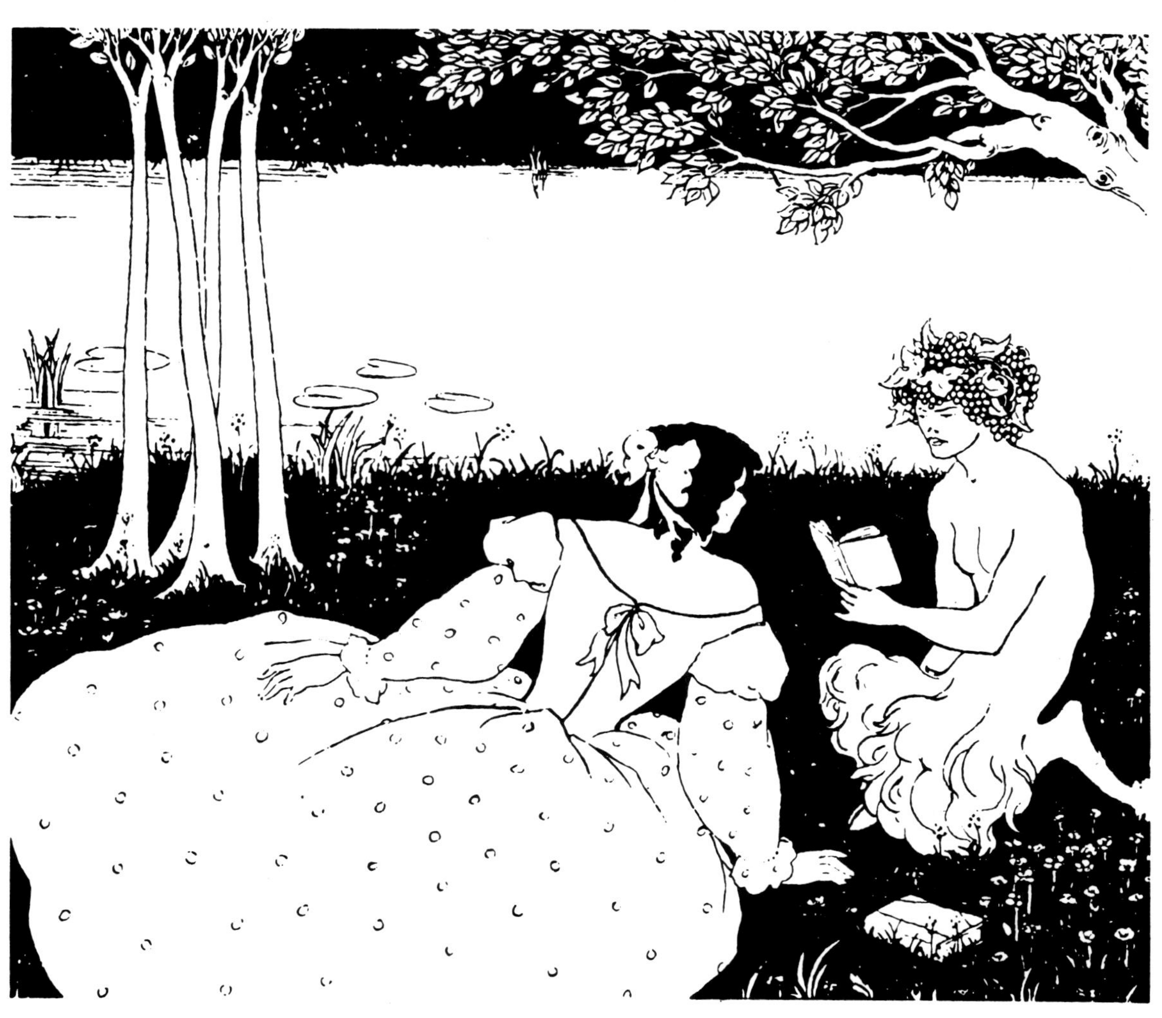

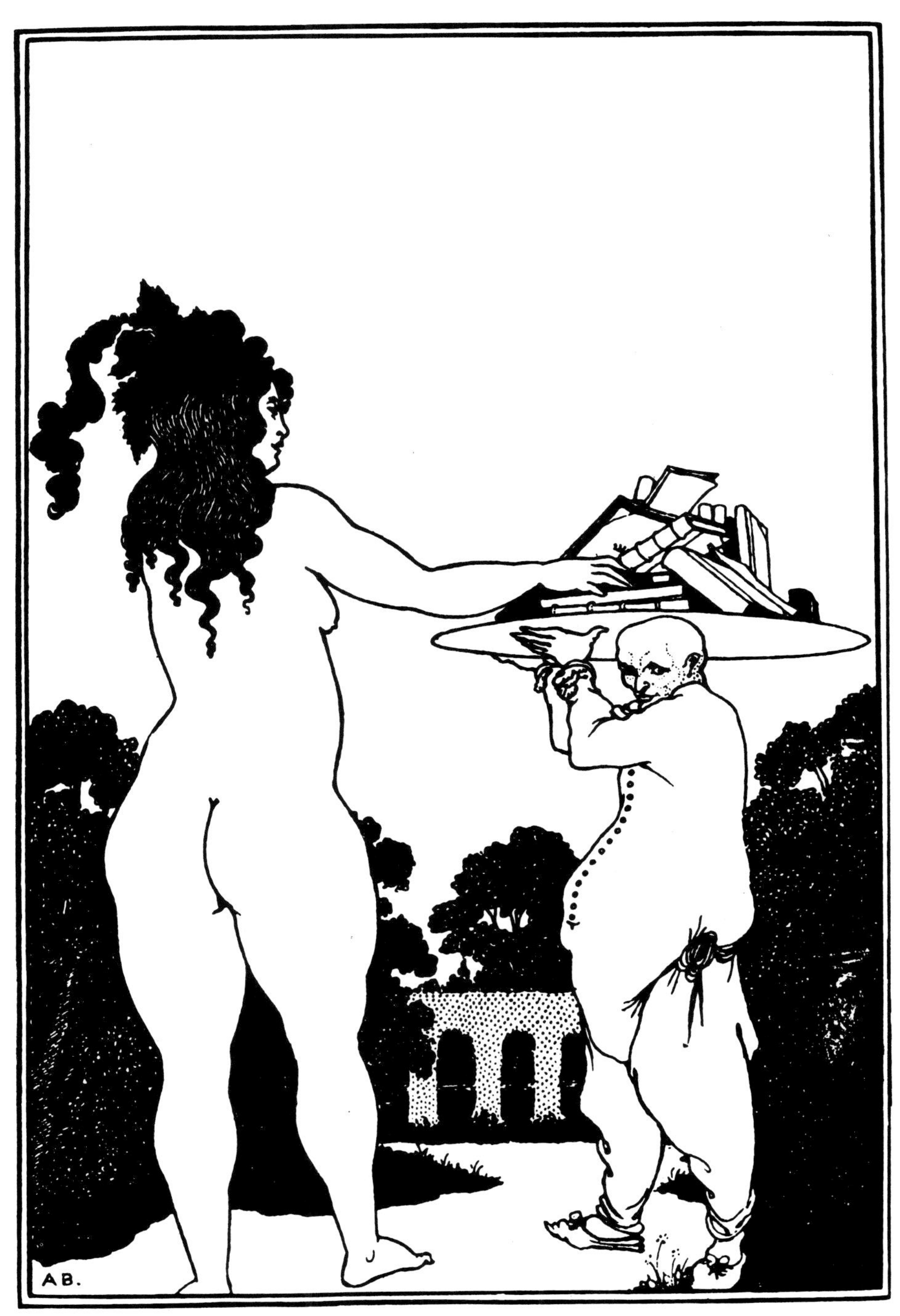

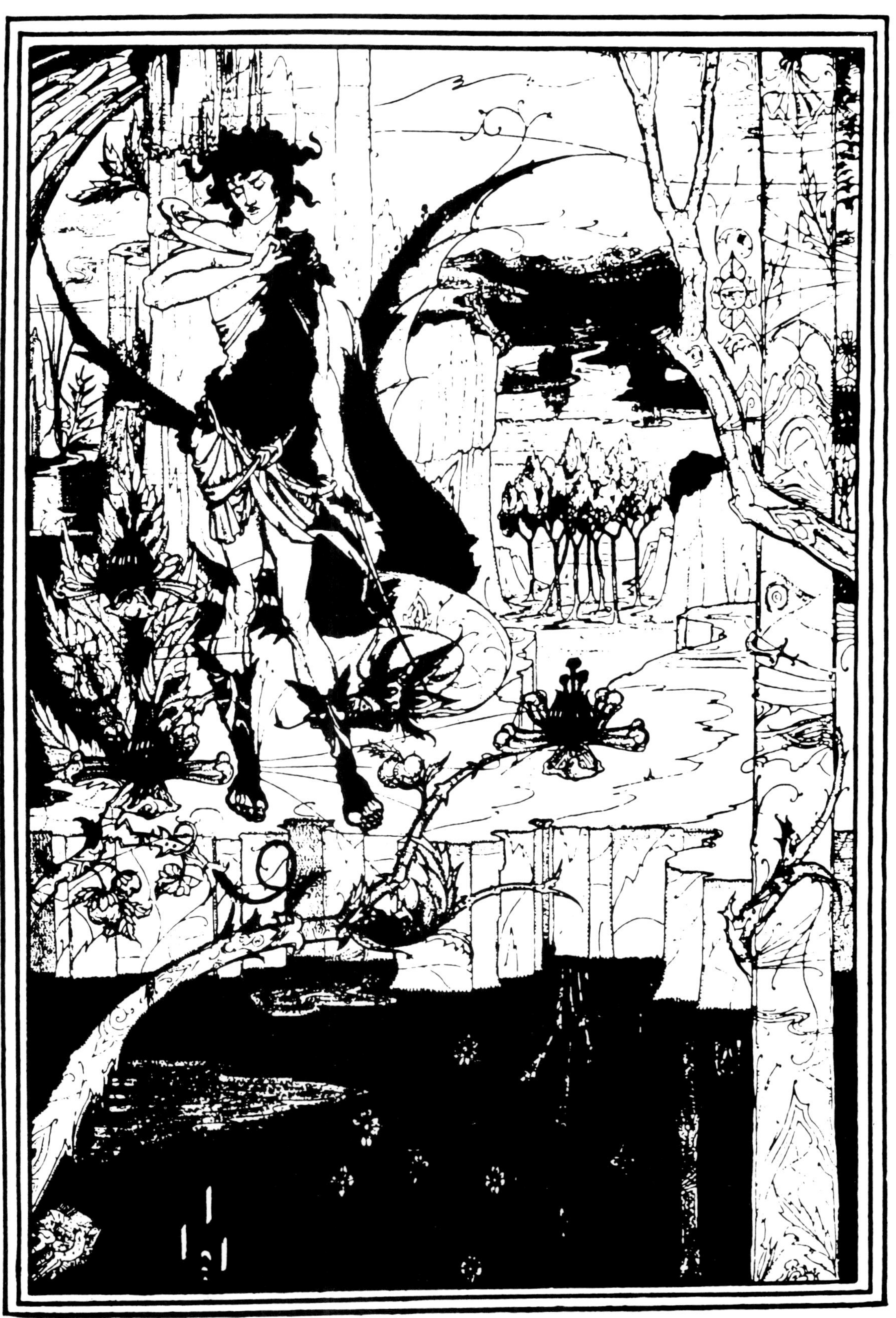

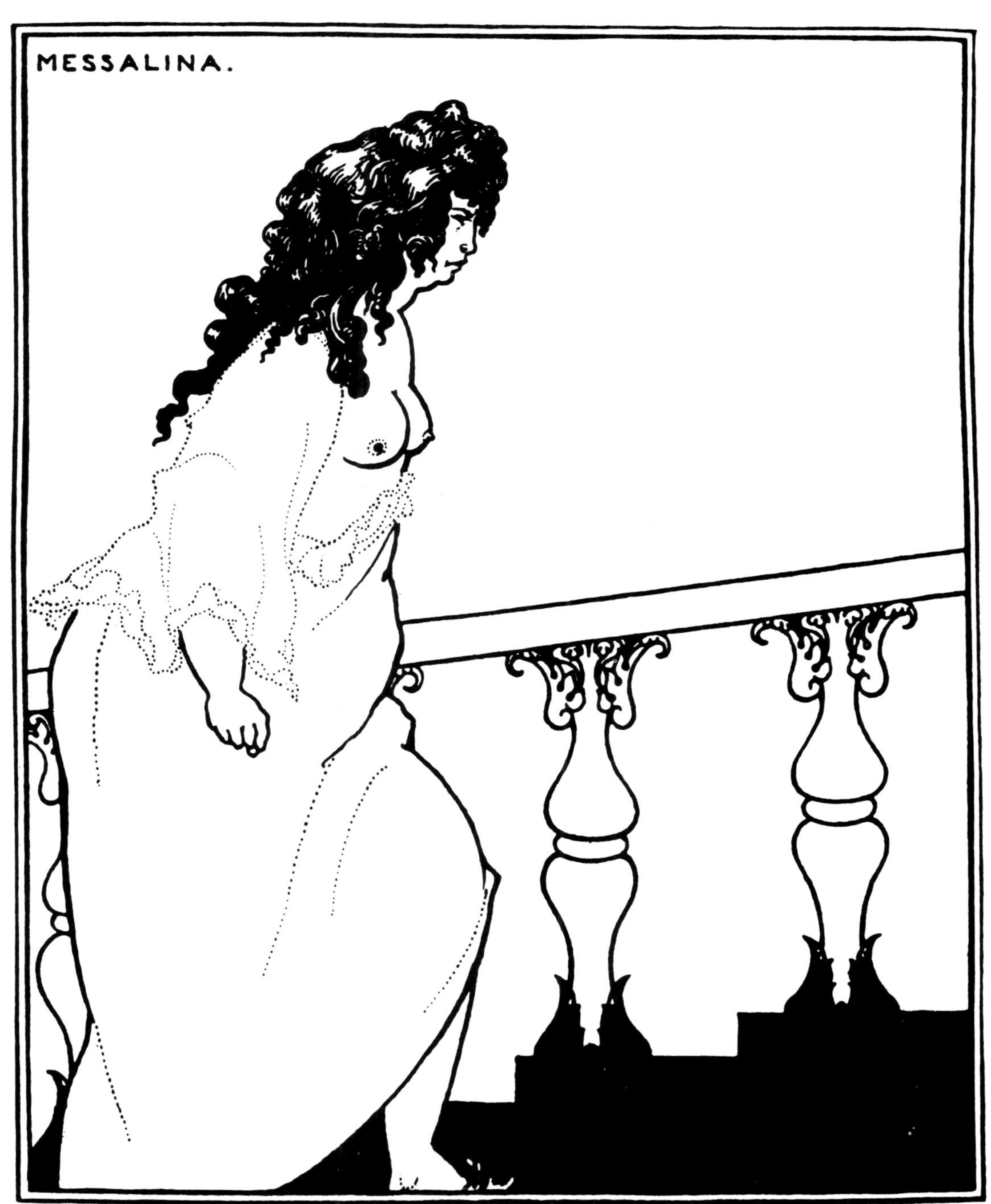
MESSALINA.

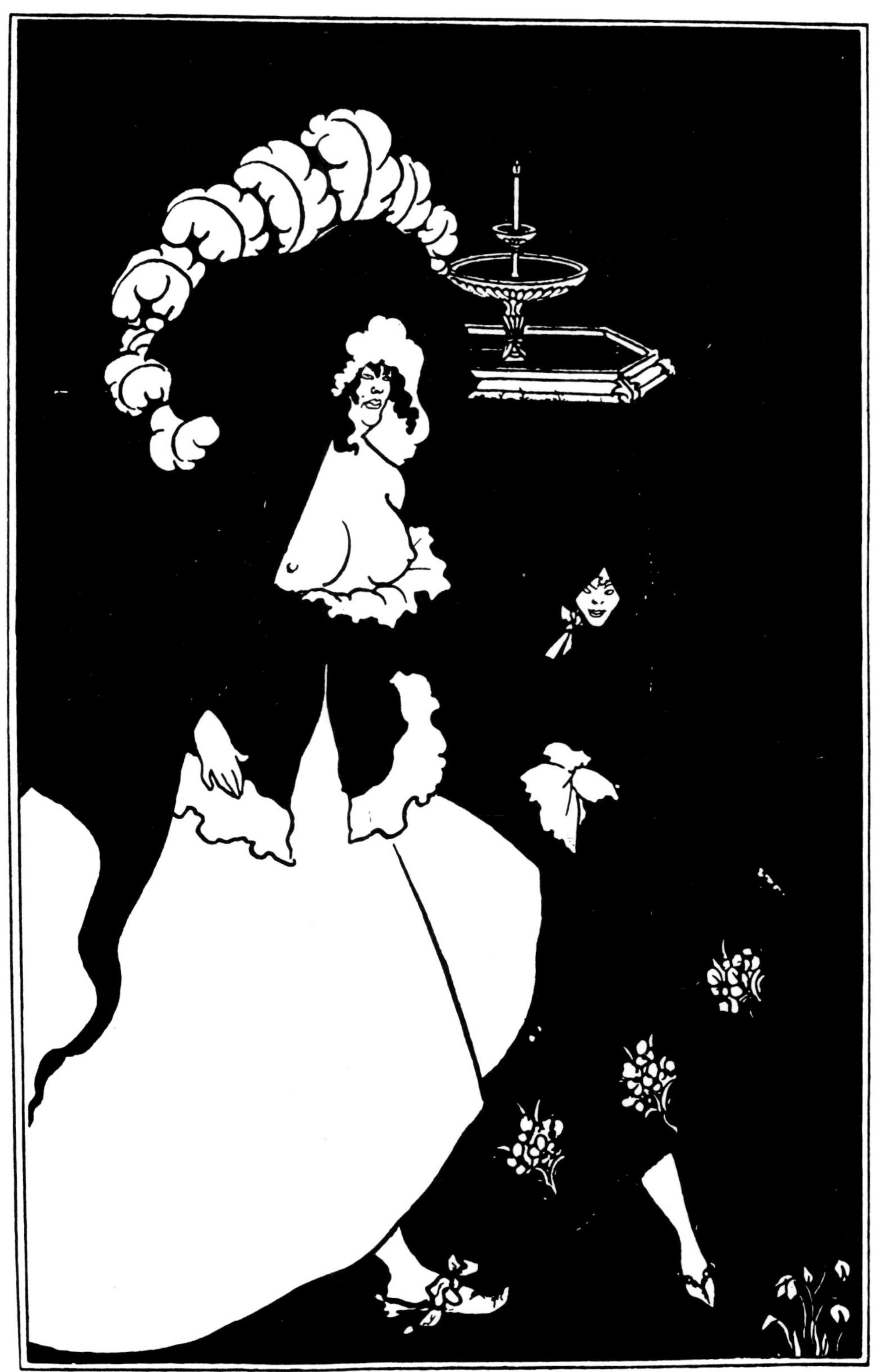

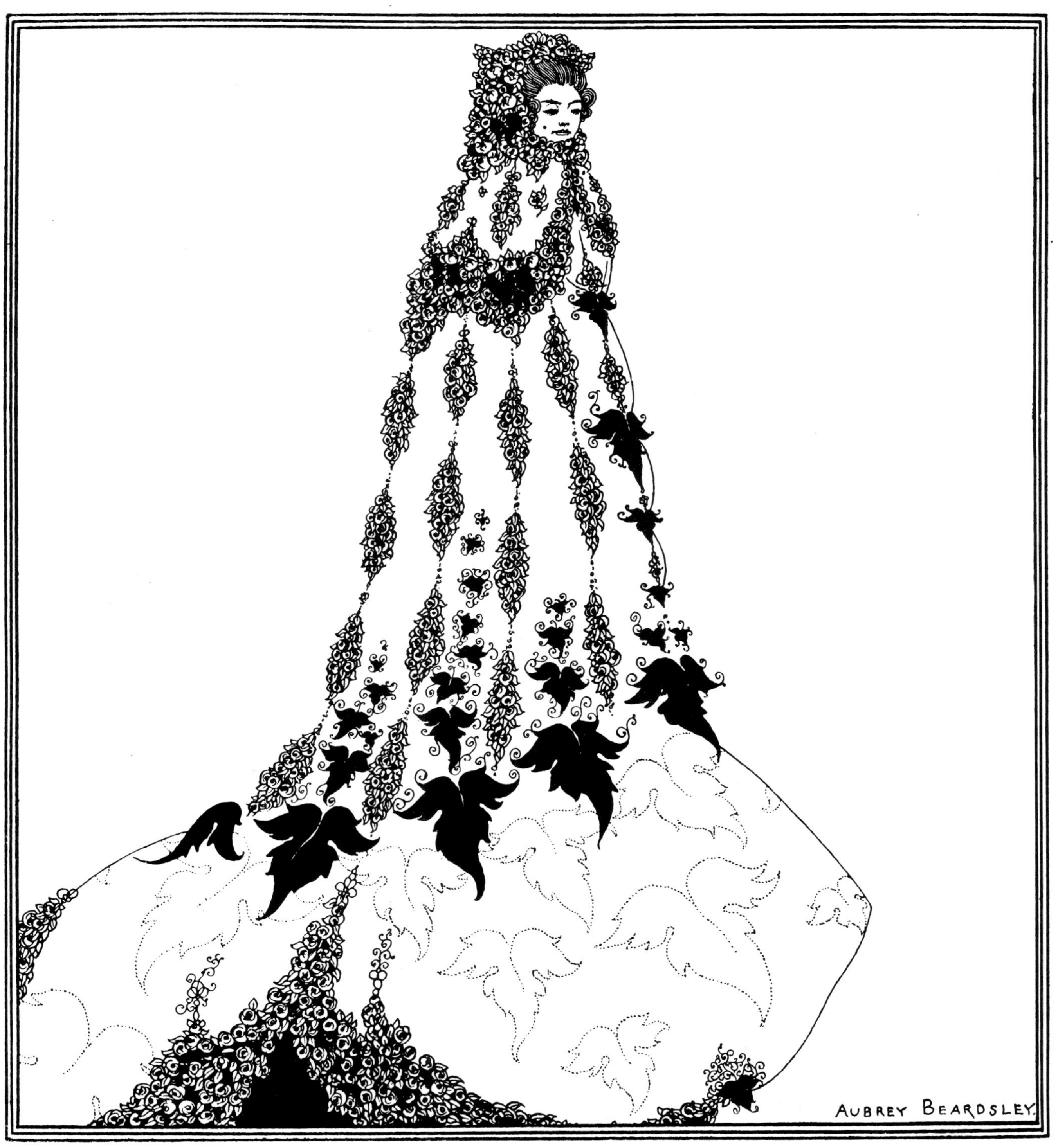
AUBREY BEARDSLEY

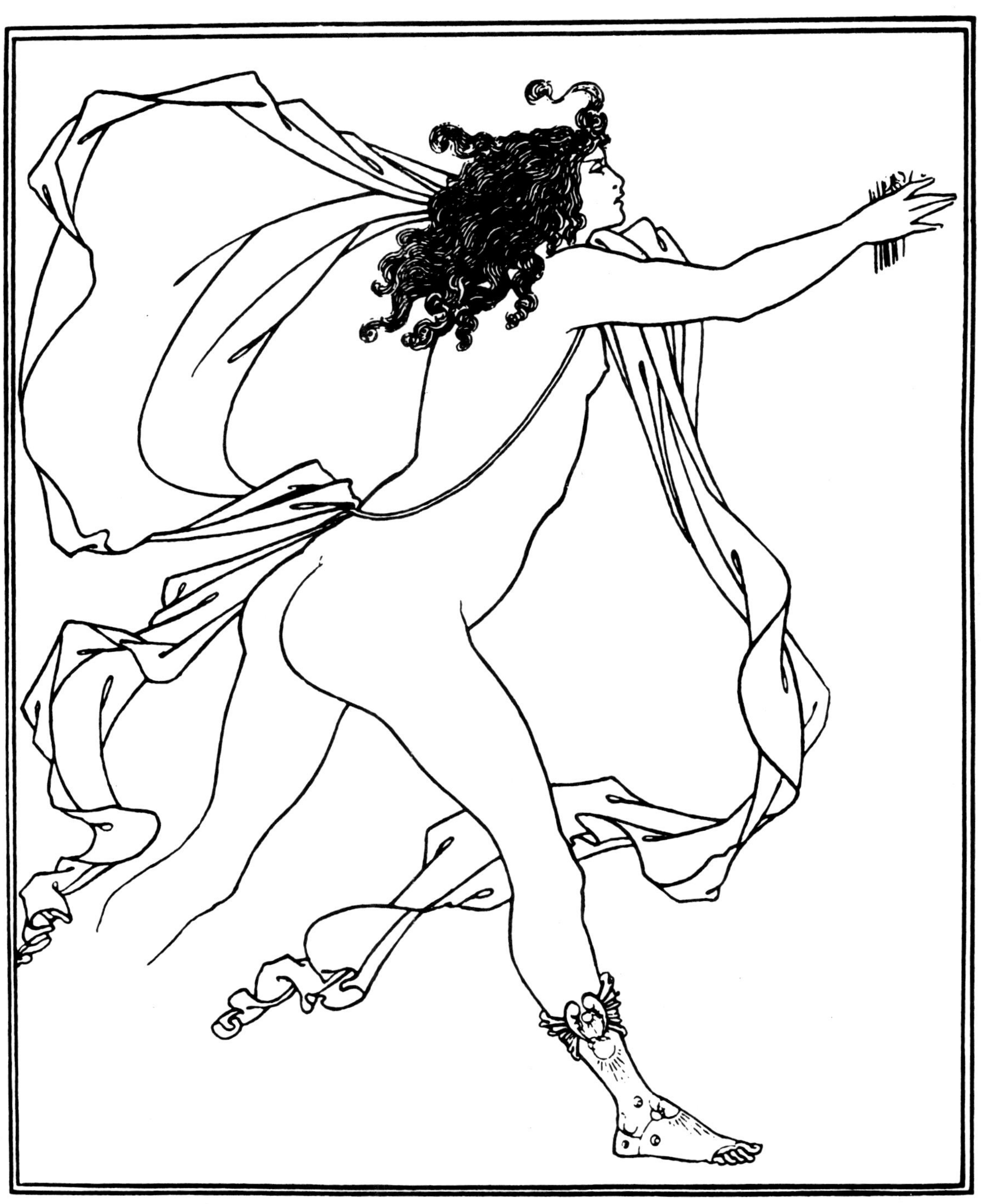

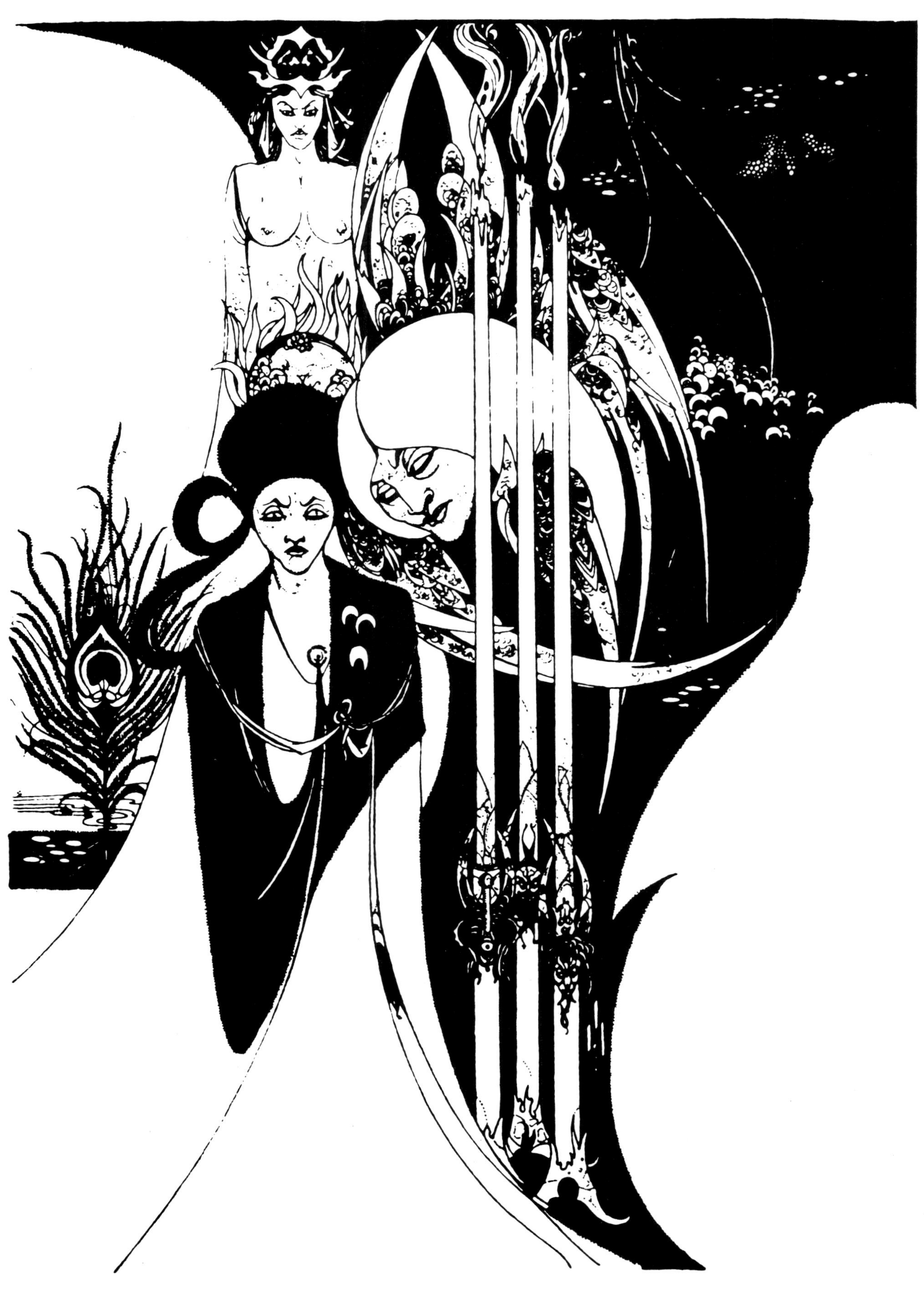

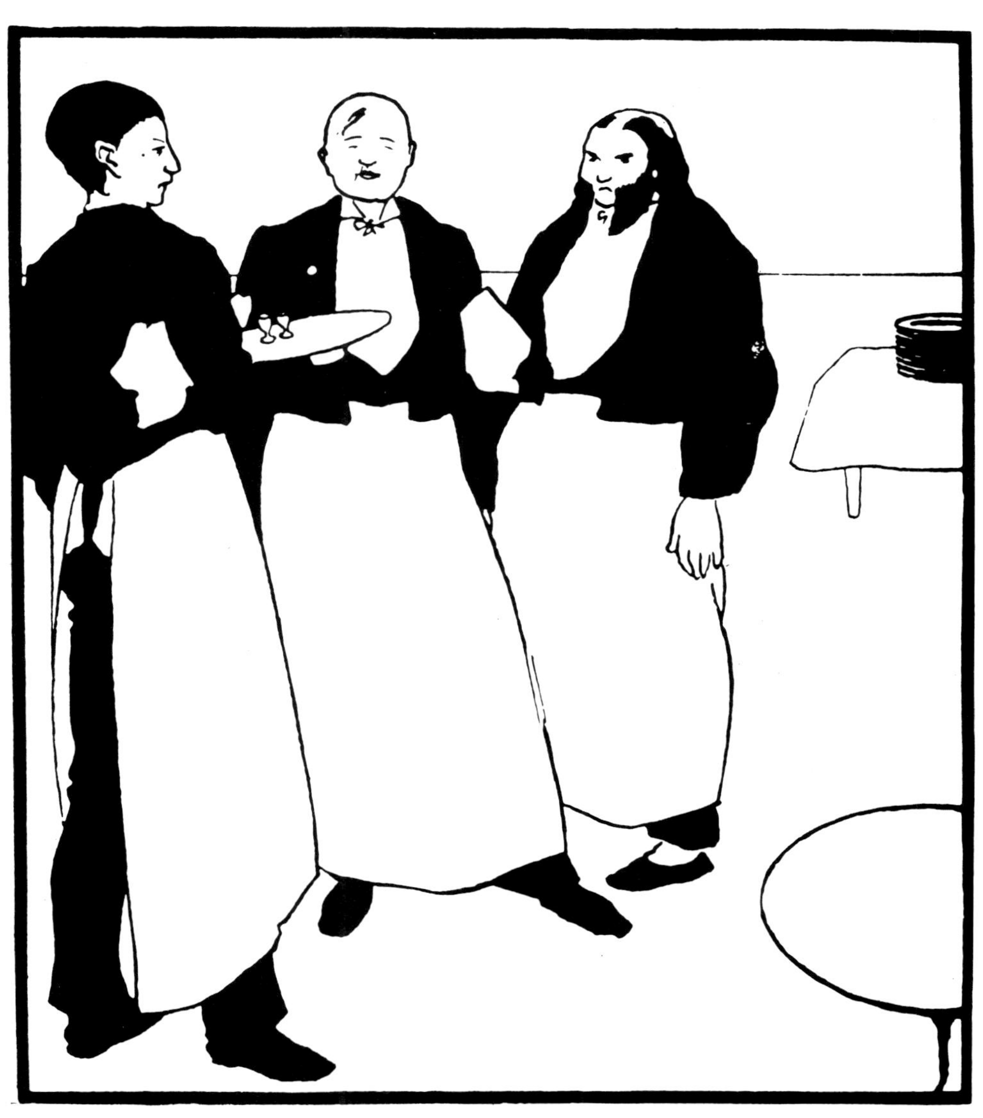

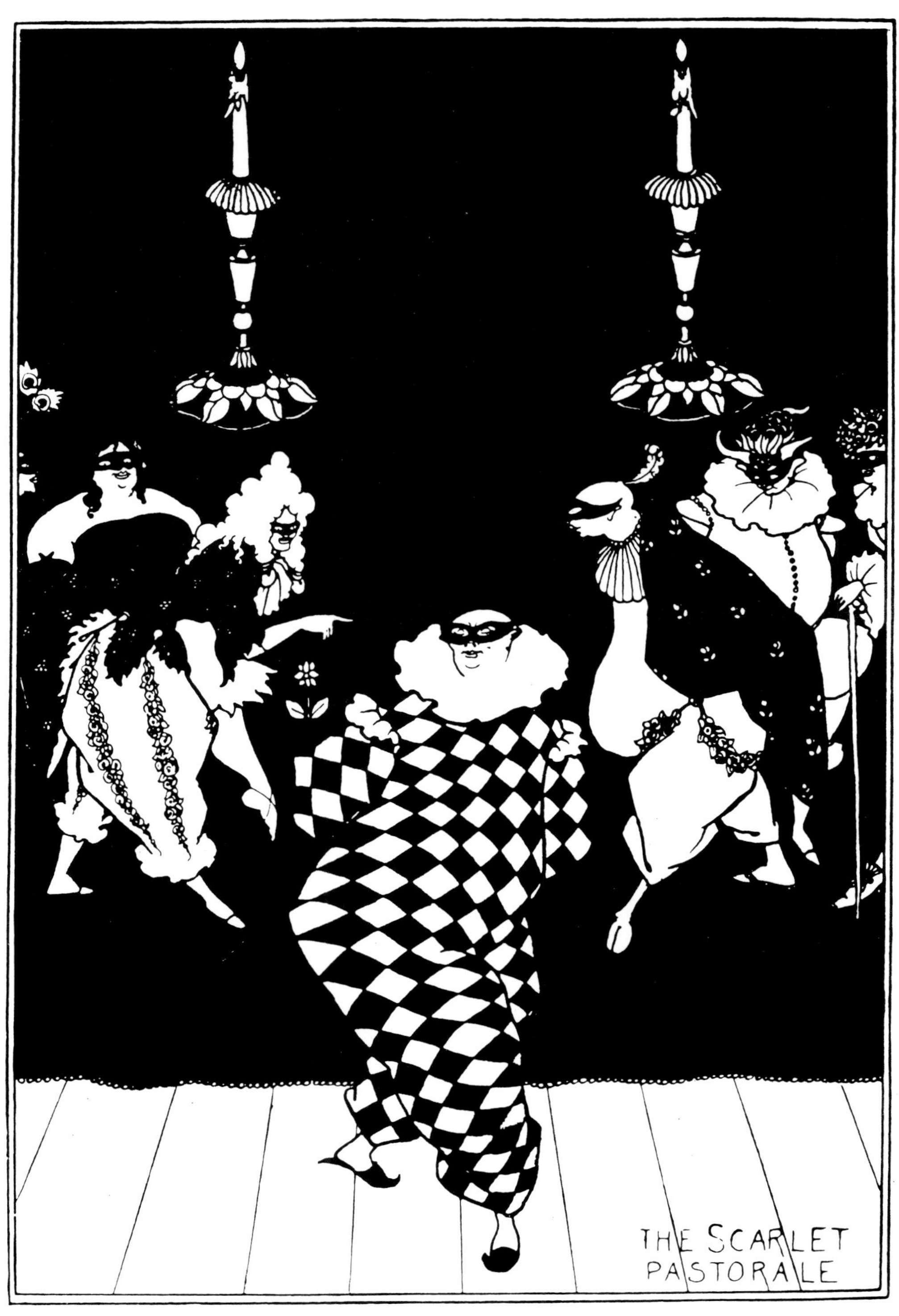
THE SCARLET
PASTORALE

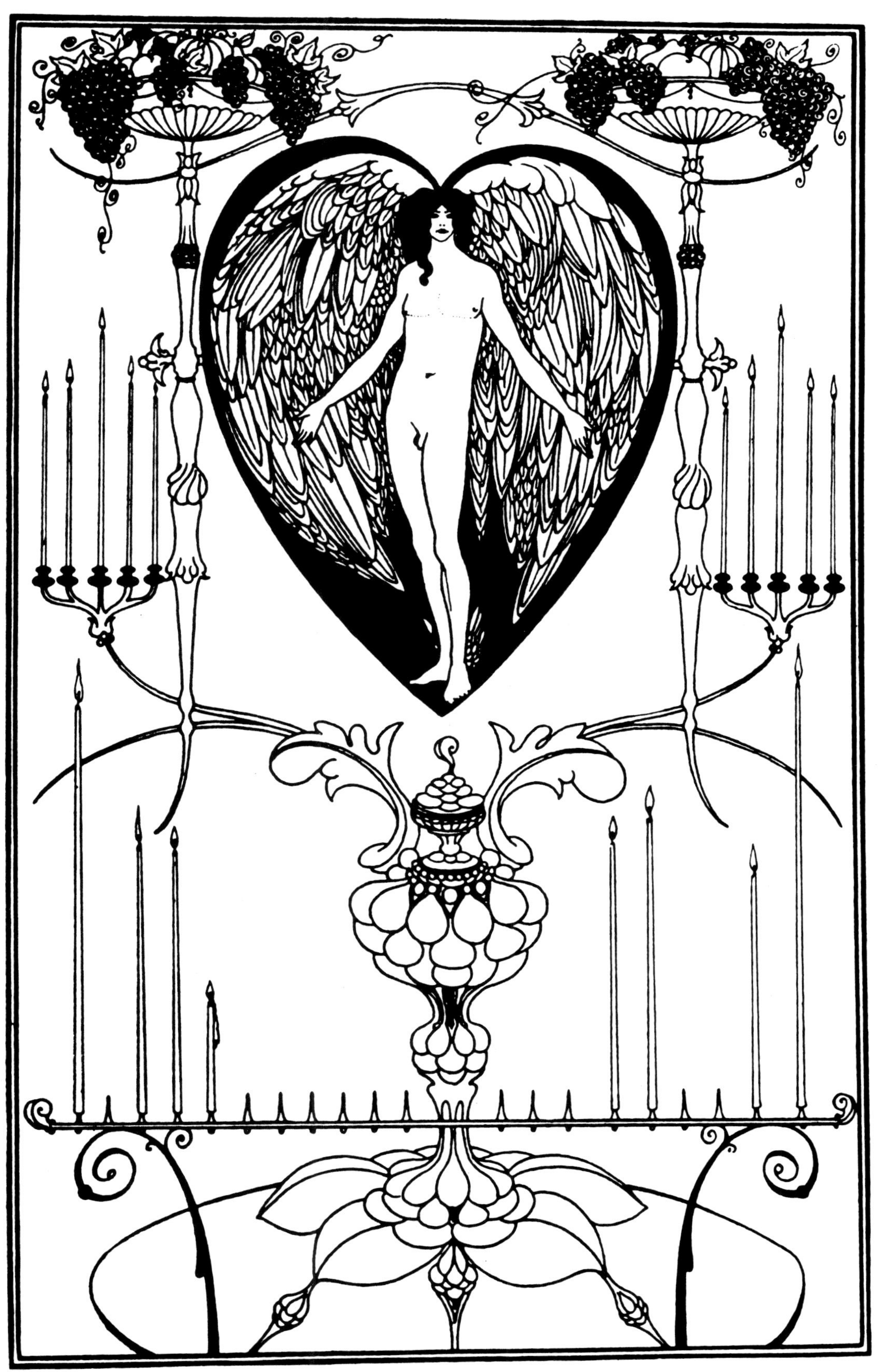

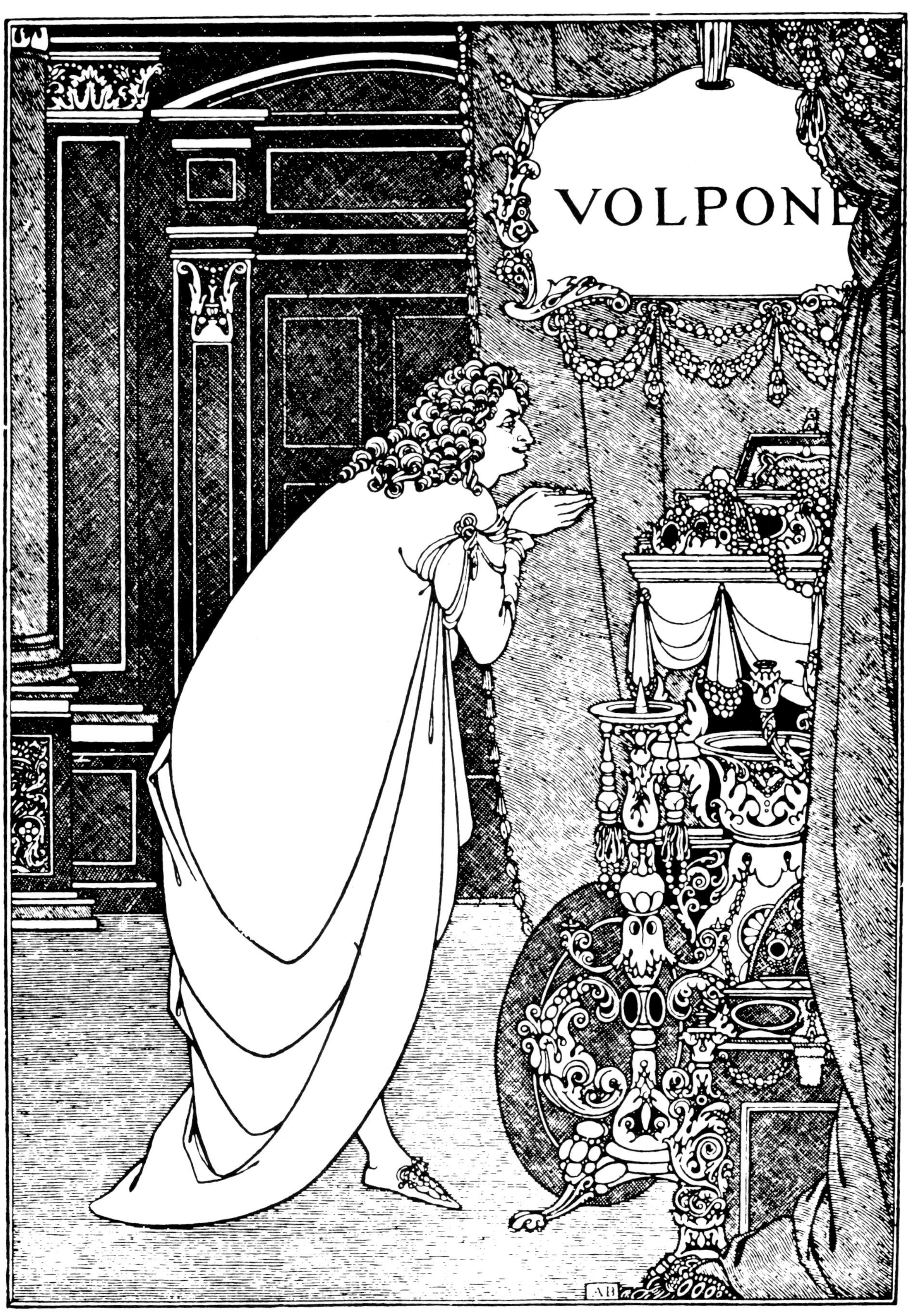
VOLPONE

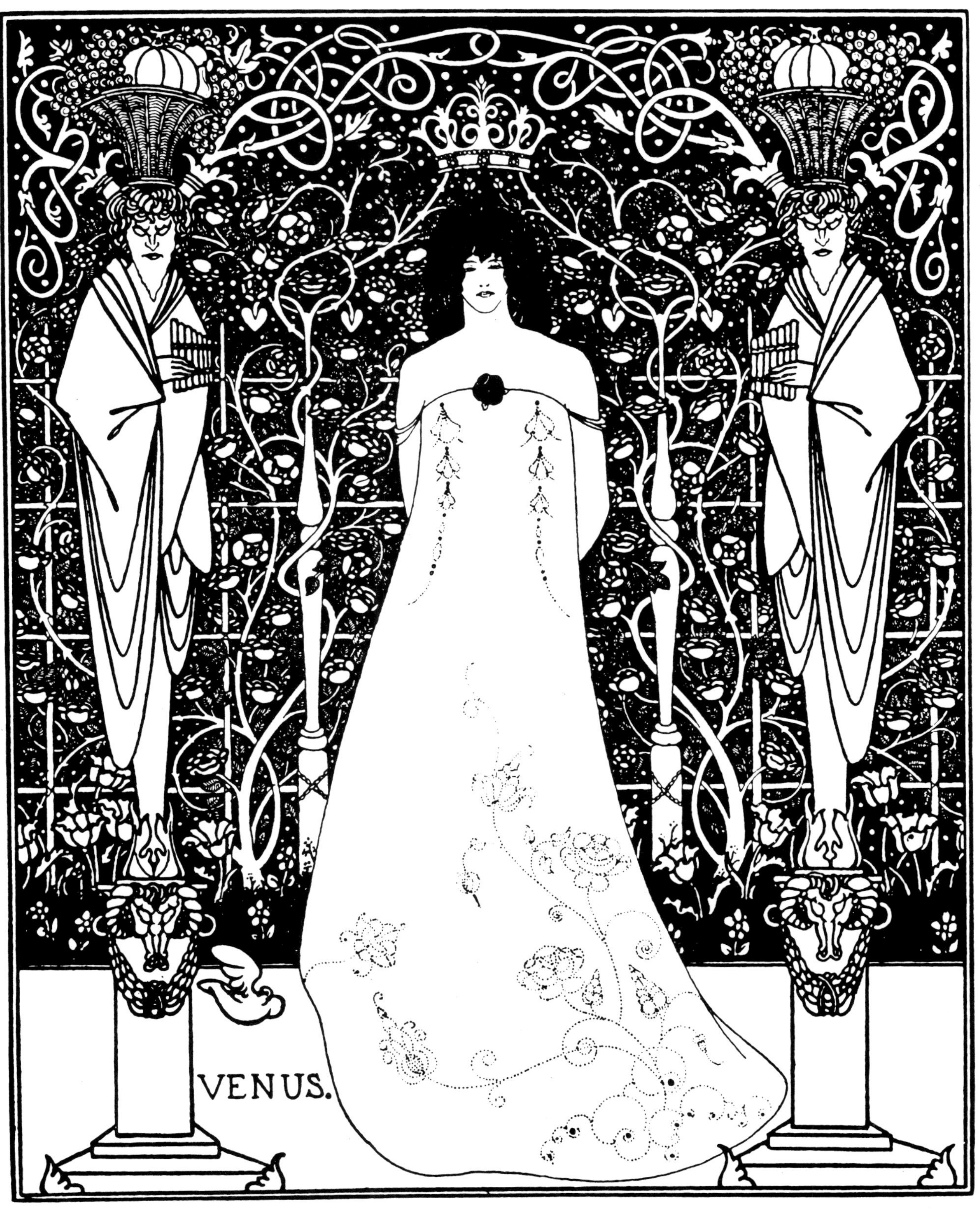
VENUS.

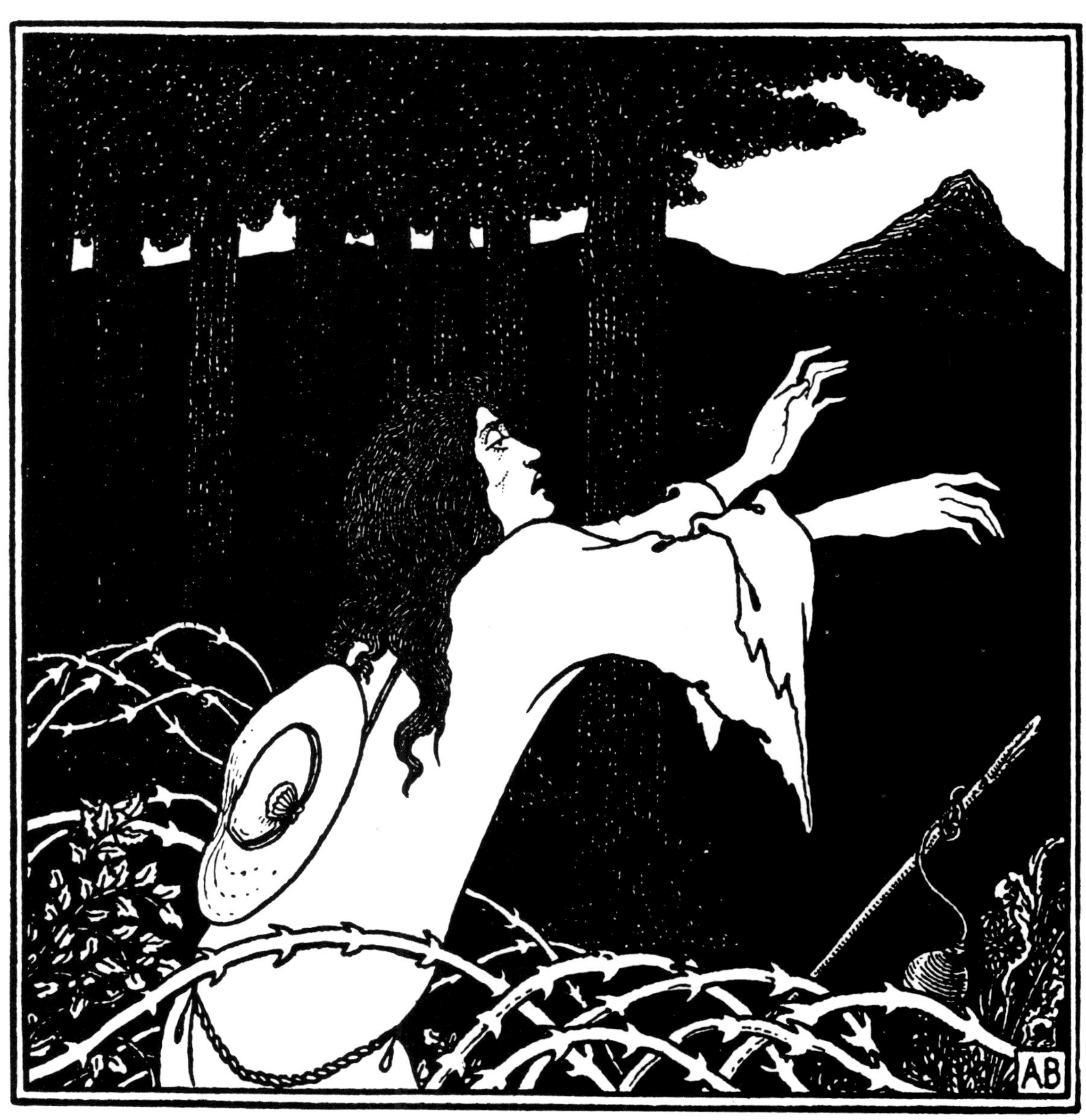

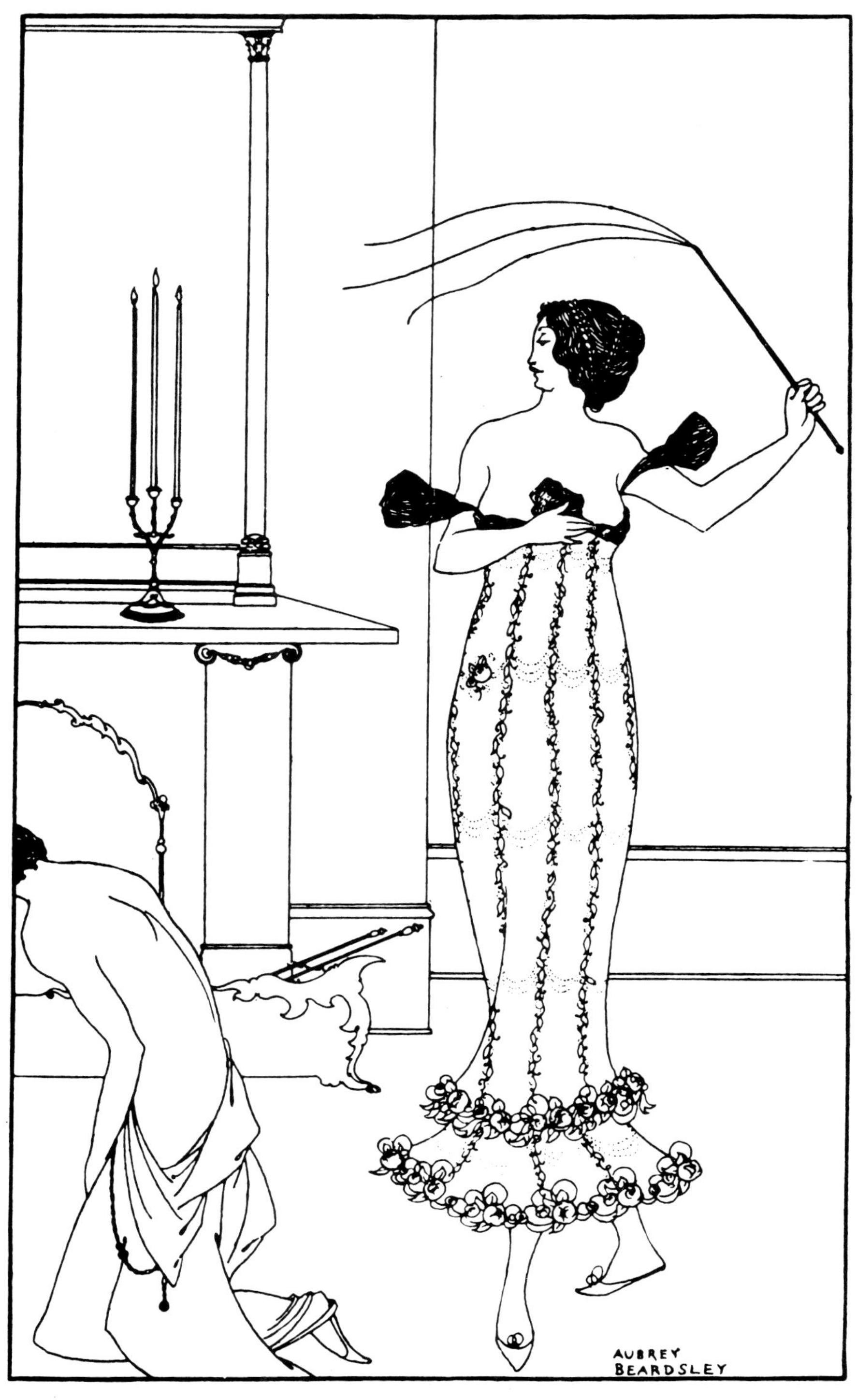
AUBREY
BEARDSLEY

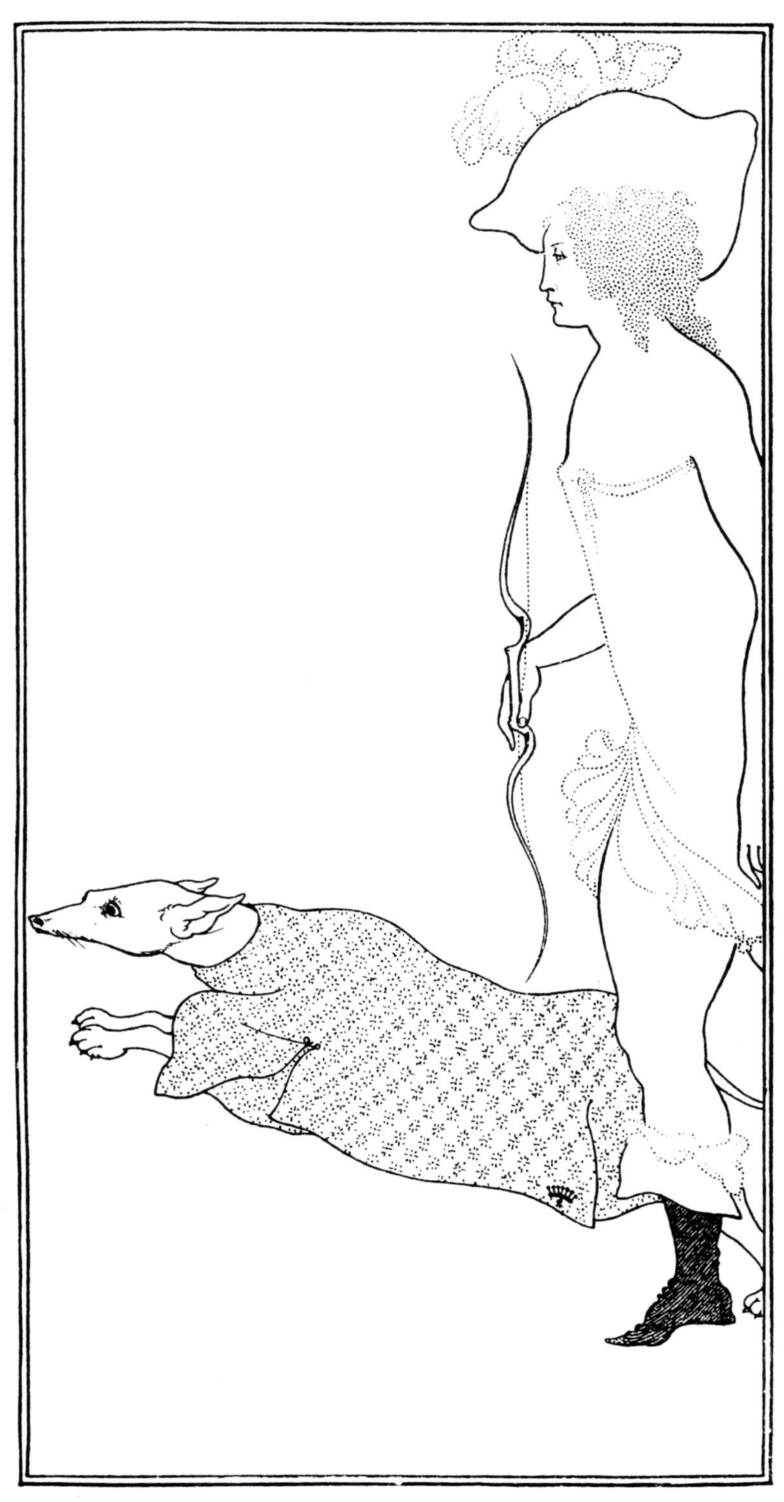

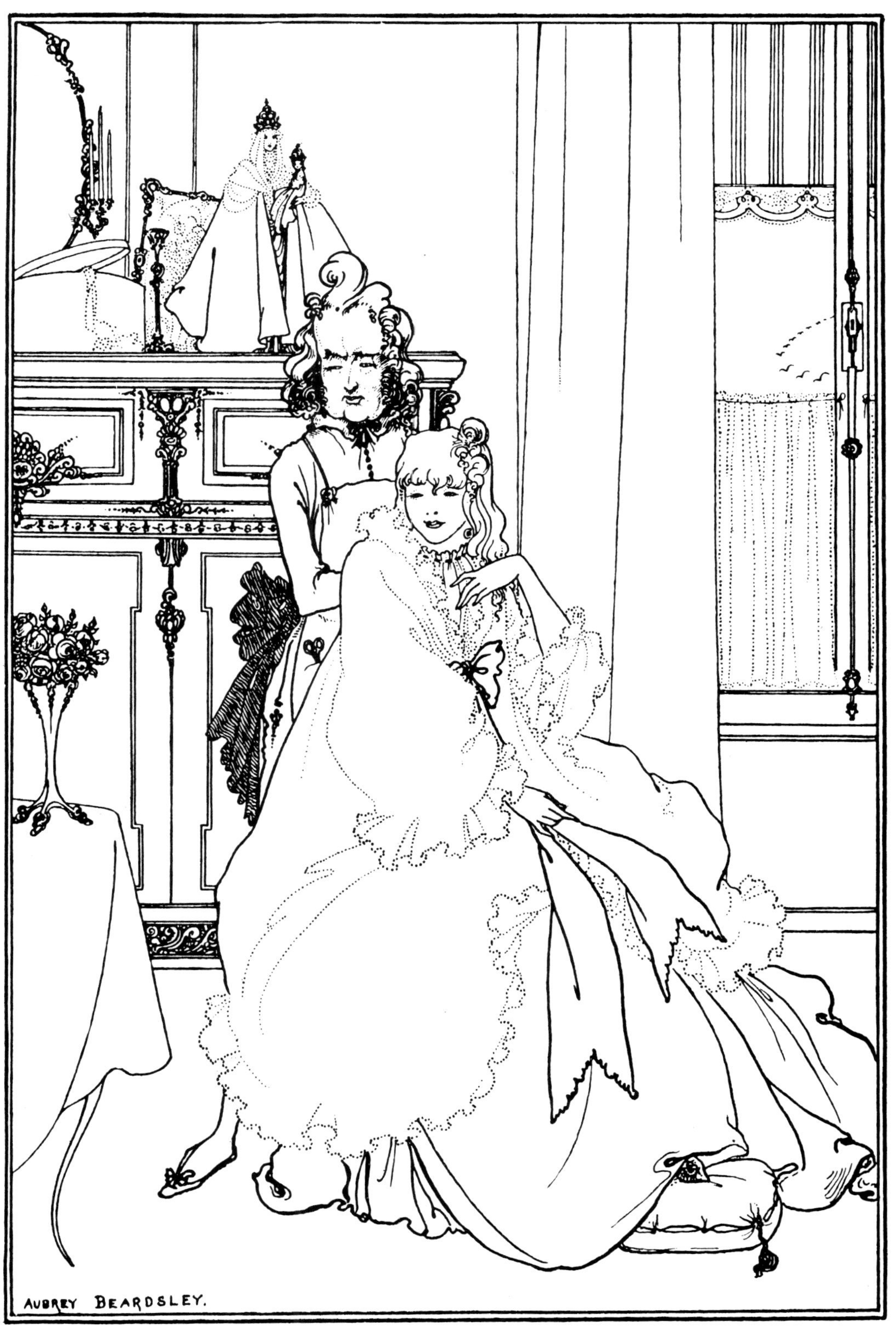
AUBREY BEARDSLEY.

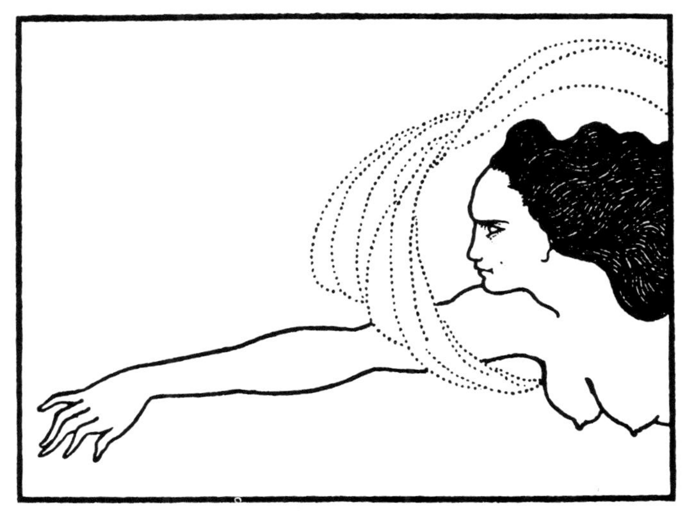

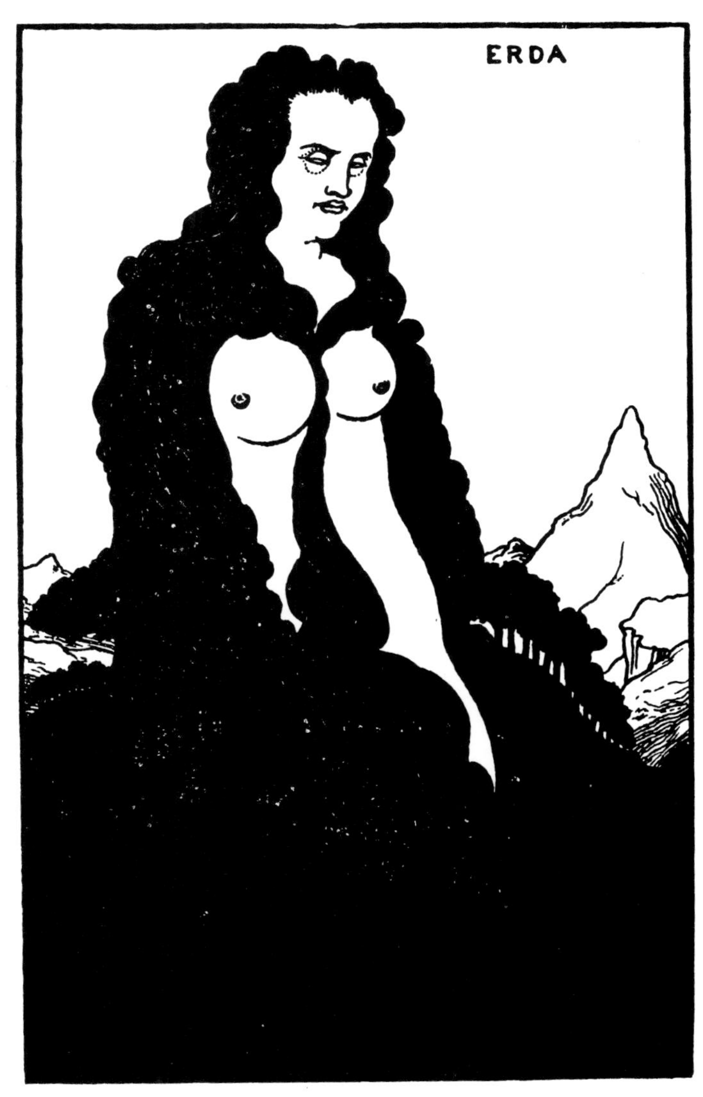

ERDA

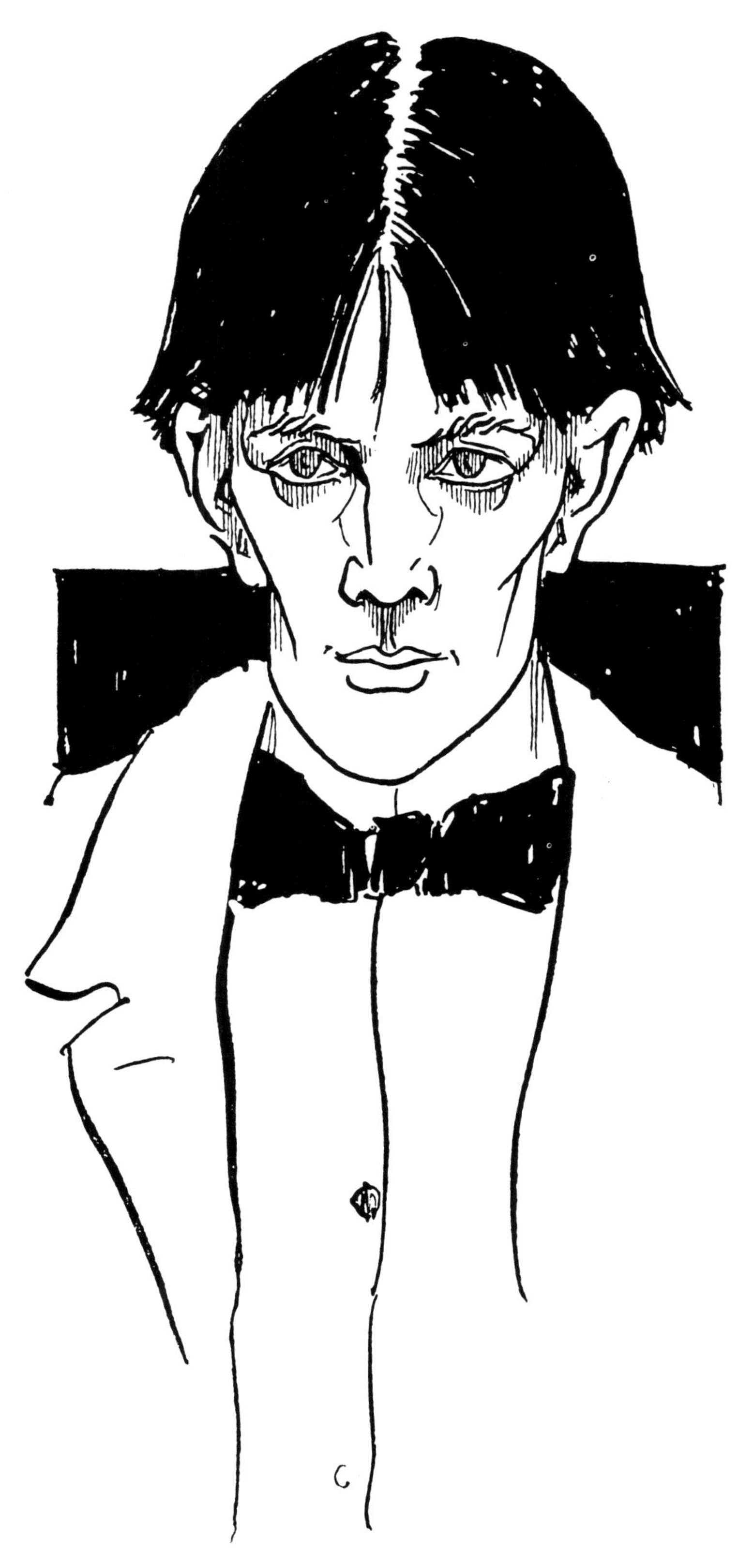